experiment
CENTRAL

experiment
CENTRAL

M-Sc volume 3

understanding scientific principles through projects

John T. Tanacredi & John Loret, General Editors

AN IMPRINT OF THE GALE GROUP

DETROIT · NEW YORK · SAN FRANCISCO
LONDON · BOSTON · WOODBRIDGE, CT

experiment
CENTRAL Understanding Scientific Principles Through Projects

Researched, developed, and illustrated by **Book Builders Incorporated**

John T. Tanacredi, *General Editor*
John Loret, *General Editor*

U•X•L Staff

Allison McNeill, *U•X•L Senior Editor*
Elizabeth Shaw, *U•X•L Associate Editor*
Carol DeKane Nagel, *U•X•L Managing Editor*
Thomas L. Romig, *U•X•L Publisher*
Meggin Condino, *Senior Analyst, New Product Development*

Shalice Shah-Caldwell, *Permissions Associate (Pictures)*

Rita Wimberley, *Senior Buyer*
Evi Seoud, *Assistant Production Manager*
Dorothy Maki, *Manufacturing Manager*
Mary Beth Trimper, *Production Director*

Eric Johnson, Tracey Rowens, *Senior Art Directors*

Pamela A. Reed, *Imaging Coordinator*
Christine O'Bryan, *Graphic Specialist*
Randy Basset, *Image Database Supervisor*
Barbara Yarrow, *Graphic Services Manager*

Linda Mahoney, LM Design, *Typesetting*

Library of Congress Cataloging-in-Publication Data.

Loret, John.
   Experiment central: understanding scientific principles through projects / John Loret,
John T. Tanacredi.
      p. cm.
   Includes bibliographical references and index.
   Contents: v. 1. A-Ec — v. 2. El-L — v. 3. M-Sc — v. 4. So-Z
   Summary: Demonstrates scientific concepts by means of experiments, including
   step-by-step instructions, lists of materials, troubleshooter's guide, and interpretation and
   explanation of results.
   ISBN 0-7876-2892-1 (set). — ISBN 0-7876-2893-X (v. 1) — ISBN 0-7876-2894-8 (v.2)
   — ISBN 0-7876-2895-6 (v.3) — ISBN 0-7876-2896-4 (v. 4)
   1. Science-Experiments-Juvenile literature. [1. Science-Experiments. 2.
   Experiments.] I. Tanacredi, John T. II. Title.
Q164 .L57 2000
507'.8-dc21   99-054142

contents

Volume 1: A-Ec

contents

experiment
CENTRAL

contents

Volume 2: El-L

contents

Volume 3: M-Sc

contents

Volume 4: So-Z

contents

reader's guide

Experiment Central: Understanding Scientific Principles Through Projects
provides in one resource a wide variety of experiments covering nine
key science curriculum fields—Astronomy, Biology, Botany,
Chemistry, Ecology, Geology, Meteorology, Physics, and Scientific
Method—spanning the earth sciences, life sciences, and physical sciences.

One hundred experiments and projects for students are presented
in 50 subject-specific chapters. Chapters, each devoted to a scientific
concept, include: Acid Rain, Biomes, Chemical Energy, Flight,
Greenhouse Effect, Optics, Solar Energy, Stars, Volcanoes, and
Weather. Two experiments or projects are provided in each chapter.

Entry format

Chapters are arranged alphabetically by scientific concept and are presented in a standard, easy-to-follow format. All chapters open with an
explanatory overview section designed to introduce students to the scientific concept and provide the background behind a concept's discovery or important figures who helped advance the study of the field.

Each experiment is divided into eight standard sections designed
to help students follow the experimental process clearly from beginning to end. Sections are:

- Purpose/Hypothesis
- Level of Difficulty
- Materials Needed
- Approximate Budget
- Timetable
- Step-by-Step Instructions
- Summary of Results
- Change the Variables

Each chapter also includes a "Design Your Own Experiment" section that allows students to apply what they have learned about a particular concept and create their own experiments. This section is divided into:

- How to Select a Topic Relating to this Concept
- Steps in the Scientific Method
- Recording Data and Summarizing the Results
- Related Projects

Concluding all chapters is a "For More Information" section that provides students with a list of books with further information about that particular topic.

Special Features

- A "Words to Know" section runs in the margin of each chapter providing definitions of terms used in that chapter. Terms in this list are bolded in the text upon first usage. A cumulative glossary collected from all "Words to Know" sections in the 50 chapters is included in the beginning of each volume.

- **Experiments by Scientific Field** index categorizes all 100 experiments by scientific curriculum area.

- **Parent's and Teacher's Guide** recommends that a responsible adult always oversee a student's experiment and provides several safety guidelines for all students to follow.

- Standard sidebar boxes accompany experiments and projects:

  "What Are the Variables?" explains the factors that may have an impact on the outcome of a particular experiment.

  "How to Experiment Safely" clearly explains any risks involved with the experiment and how to avoid them. While all experiments have been constructed with safety in mind, it is always recommended to proceed with caution and work under adult supervision while performing any experiment (please refer to Parent's and Teacher's Guide on page xvii).

  "Troubleshooter's Guide" presents problems that a student might encounter with an experiment, possible causes of the problem, and ways to remedy the problem.

- **Budget Index** categorizes experiments by approximate cost. Budgets may vary depending on what materials are readily available in the average household.

- **Level of Difficulty Index** lists experiments according to "Easy," "Moderate," "Difficult," or combination thereof. Level of difficulty is determined by such factors as the time necessary to complete the experiment, level of adult supervision recommended, and skill level of the average student. Level of difficulty will vary depending on the student. A teacher or parent should always be consulted before any experiment is attempted.

- **Timetable Index** categorizes each experiment by the time needed to complete it, including set-up and follow-through time. Times given are approximate.

- **General Subject Index** provides access to all major terms, people, places, and topics covered in *Experiment Central.*

- Approximately **150 photographs** enhance the text.

- Approximately **300 drawings** illustrate specific steps in the experiments, helping students follow the experimental procedure.

Acknowledgments

Credit is due to the general editors of *Experiment Central* who lent their time and expertise to the project, and oversaw compilation of the volumes and their contents:

John T. Tanacredi, Ph.D.
Adjunct Full Professor of Ecology
Department of Civil and Environmental Engineering,
Polytechnic University
Adjunct Full Professor of Environmental Sciences,
Nassau Community College, State University of New York
President, The Science Museum of Long Island

John Loret, Ph.D., D.Sc.
Professor Emeritus and Former Director of Environmental
Studies of Queens College, City University of New York
Director, The Science Museum of Long Island

A note of appreciation is extended to the *Experiment Central* advisors, who provided their input when this work was in its formative stages:

Linda Barr
Editor and Writer for Book Builders Incorporated

Teresa F. Bettac
Middle School Advanced Science Teacher
Delaware, Ohio

Linda Leuzzi
Writer, Trustee of The Science Museum of Long Island

David J. Miller
Director of Education
The Science Museum of Long Island

Gracious thanks are also extended to science copyeditor Chris Cavette for his invaluable comments, expertise, and dedication to the project.

Comments and Suggestions

We welcome your comments on *Experiment Central*. Please write: Editors, *Experiment Central,* U•X•L, 27500 Drake Rd., Farmington Hills, Michigan, 48331–3535; call toll free: 1–800–877–4253; fax: 248–414–5043; or send e-mail via http://www.galegroup.com.

parent's and teacher's guide

The experiments and projects in *Experiment Central* have been carefully constructed with issues of safety in mind, but your guidance and supervision are still required. Following the safety guidelines that accompany each experiment and project (found in the "How to Experiment Safely" sidebar box), as well as putting to work the safe practices listed below, will help your child or student avoid accidents. Oversee your child or student during experiments, and make sure he or she follows these safety guidelines:

- Always wear safety goggles if there is any possibility of sharp objects, small particles, splashes of liquid, or gas fumes getting in someone's eyes.

- Always wear protective gloves when handling materials that could irritate the skin.

- Never leave an open flame, such as a lit candle, unattended. Never wear loose clothing around an open flame.

- Follow instructions carefully when using electrical equipment, including batteries, to avoid getting shocked.

- Be cautious when handling sharp objects or glass equipment that might break. Point scissors away from you and use them carefully.

- Always ask for help in cleaning up spills, broken glass, or other hazardous materials.

- Always use protective gloves when handling hot objects. Set them down only on a protected surface that will not be damaged by heat.

- Always wash your hands thoroughly after handling material that might contain harmful microorganisms, such as soil and pond water.

- Do not substitute materials in an experiment without asking a knowledgeable adult about possible reactions.

- Do not use or mix unidentified liquids or powders. The result might be an explosion or poisonous fumes.

- Never taste or eat any substances being used in an experiment.

- Always wear old clothing or a protective apron to avoid staining your clothes.

experiments by scientific field

Chapter name in
brackets, followed
by experiment name;
bold type indicates
volume number, followed
by page number.

Chemistry

Ecology

All Subjects

experiments by scientific field

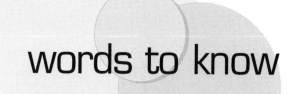

words to know

A

Abscission: The point at which a leaf meets a twig.

Acceleration: The rate at which the velocity and/or direction of an object is changing with the respect to time.

Acid: Substance that when dissolved in water is capable of reacting with a base to form salts and release hydrogen ions.

Acid rain: A form of precipitation that is significantly more acidic than neutral water, often produced as the result of industrial processes.

Acoustics: The science concerned with the production, properties, and propagation of sound waves.

Active solar energy system: A solar energy system that uses pumps or fans to circulate heat captured from the Sun.

Adhesion: Attraction between two different substances.

Aeration: Shaking a liquid to allow trapped gases to escape and to add oxygen.

Aerobic: Requiring oxygen.

Aerodynamics: The study of the motion of gases (particularly air) and the motion and control of objects in the air.

Alga/Algae: Single-celled or multicellular plants or plantlike organisms that contain chlorophyll, thus making their own food by photosynthesis. Algae grow mainly in water.

Alignment: Adjustment to a certain direction or orientation.

Alkaline: Having a pH of more than 7.

Alloy: A mixture of two or more metals with properties different from those metals of which it is made.

Amine: An organic compound derived from ammonia.

Amphibians: Animals that live on land and breathe air but return to the water to reproduce.

Amplitude: The maximum displacement (difference between an original position and a later position) of the material that is vibrating. Amplitude can be thought of visually as the highest and lowest points of a wave.

Anaerobic: Functioning without oxygen.

Anemometer: A device that measures wind speed.

Animalcules: Life forms that Anton van Leeuwenhoek named when he first saw them under his microscope; they later became known as protozoa and bacteria.

Anthocyanin: Red pigment found in leaves, petals, stems, and other parts of a plant.

Antibody: A protein produced by certain cells of the body as an immune (disease-fighting) response to a specific foreign antigen.

Aquifer: Underground layer of sand, gravel, or spongy rock that collects water.

Arch: A curved structure spanning an opening that supports a wall or other weight above the opening.

Artesian well: A well in which water is under pressure.

Asexual reproduction: Any reproductive process that does not involve the union of two individuals in the exchange of genetic material.

Astronomers: Scientists who study the positions, motions, and composition of stars and other objects in the sky.

Astronomy: The study of the physical properties of objects and matter outside Earth's atmosphere.

Atmosphere: Layers of air that surround Earth.

Atmospheric pressure: The pressure exerted by the atmosphere at Earth's surface due to the weight of the air.

Atom: The smallest unit of an element, made up of protons and neutrons in a central nucleus surrounded by moving electrons.

Autotroph: An organism that can build all the food and produce all the energy it needs with its own resources.

Auxins: A group of plant hormones responsible for patterns of plant growth.

B

Bacteria: Single-celled microorganisms that live in soil, water, plants, and animals that play a key role in the decaying of organic matter and the cycling of nutrients. Some are agents of disease.

Bacteriology: The scientific study of bacteria, their characteristics, and their activities as related to medicine, industry, and agriculture.

Base: Substance that when dissolved in water is capable of reacting with an acid to form salts and release hydrogen ions; has a pH of more than 7.

Beriberi: A disease caused by a deficiency of thiamine and characterized by nerve and gastrointestinal disorders.

Biochemical oxygen demand (BOD$_5$): The amount of oxygen that microorganisms use over a five-day period in 68° Fahrenheit (20° Celsius) water to decay organic matter.

Biological variables: Living factors such as bacteria, fungi, and animals that can affect the processes that occur in nature and in an experiment.

Biomes: Large geographical areas with specific climates and soils, as well as distinct plant and animal communities that are interdependent.

Bond: The force that holds two atoms together.

Botany: The branch of biology involving the study of plant life.

Braided rivers: Wide, shallow rivers with pebbly islands in the middle.

Buoyancy: The tendency of a fluid to exert a lifting effect on a body immersed in it.

By-products: Something produced in the making of something else.

C

Calibration: Standardizing or adjusting a measuring instrument so its measurements are correct.

Capillary action: The tendency of water to rise through a narrow tube by the force of adhesion between the water and the walls of the tube.

Carbohydrate: A compound consisting of carbon, hydrogen, and oxygen found in plants and used as a food by humans and other animals.

Carnivore: Meat-eating organism.

Carotene: Yellowish-orange pigment present in most leaves.

Catalyst: A compound that speeds up the rate of a chemical reaction without undergoing any change in its own composition.

Celestial: Describing planets or other objects in space.

Cell: The basic unit of a living organism; cells are structured to perform highly specialized functions.

Cell membrane: The thin layer of tissue that surrounds a cell.

Cell theory: The idea that all living things have one or more similar cells that carry out the same functions for the living process.

Centrifuge: A device that rapidly spins a solution so that the heavier components will separate from the lighter ones.

Centripetal force: Rotating force that moves towards the center or axis.

Channel: A shallow trench carved into the ground by the pressure and movement of a river.

Chemical energy: Energy stored in chemical bonds.

Chemical property: A characteristic of a substance that allows it to undergo a chemical change. Chemical properties include flammability and sensitivity to light.

Chemical reaction: Any chemical change in which at least one new substance is formed.

Chlorophyll: A green pigment found in plants that absorbs sunlight, providing the energy used in photosynthesis, or the conversion of carbon dioxide and water to complex carbohydrates.

Chloroplasts: Small structures in plant cells that contain chlorophyll and in which the process of photosynthesis takes place.

Chromatography: A method for separating mixtures into their component parts (into their "ingredients," or into what makes them up).

Circuit: The complete path of an electric current including the source of electric energy.

Cleavage: The tendency of a mineral to split along certain planes.

Climate: The average weather that a region experiences over a long period.

Coagulation: The clumping together of particles in a liquid.

Cohesion: Attraction between like substances.

Colloid: A mixture containing particles suspended in, but not dissolved in, a dispersing medium.

Colony: A mass of microorganisms that have been bred in a medium.

Combustion: Any chemical reaction in which heat, and usually light, is produced. It is commonly the burning of organic substances during which oxygen from the air is used to form carbon dioxide and water vapor.

Complete metamorphosis: Metamorphosis in which a larva becomes a pupa before changing into an adult form.

Composting: The process in which organic compounds break down and become dark, fertile soil called humus.

Concave: Hollowed or rounded upward, like the inside of a bowl; arched.

Concentration: The amount of a substance present in a given volume, such as the number of molecules in a liter.

Condense/condensation: The process by which a gas changes into a liquid.

Conduction: The flow of heat through a solid.

Confined aquifer: An aquifer with a layer of impermeable rock above it; the water is held under pressure.

Coniferous: Refers to trees, such as pines and firs, that bear cones and have needle-like leaves that are not shed all at once.

Constellations: Eighty-eight patterns of stars in the night sky.

Continental drift: The theory that continents move apart slowly at a predictable rate.

Control experiment: A set-up that is identical to the experiment but is not affected by the variable that will be changed during the experiment.

Convection: The circulatory motion that occurs in a gas or liquid at a nonuniform temperature; the variation of the motion is caused by the substance's density and the action of gravity.

Convection current: Circular movement of a fluid in response to alternating heating and cooling.

Convex: Curved or rounded like the outside of a ball.

Corona: The outermost atmospheric layer of the Sun.

Corrosion: An oxidation-reduction reaction in which a metal is oxidized (reacted with oxygen) and oxygen is reduced, usually in the presence of moisture.

Cotyledon: Seed leaves, which contain stored food for the embryo.

Crust: The hard, outer shell of Earth that floats upon the softer, denser mantle.

Cultures: Microorganisms growing in prepared nutrients.

Cyanobacteria: Oxygen-producing, aquatic bacteria capable of manufacturing its own food; resembles algae.

Cycle: Occurrence of events that take place the same time every year; a single complete vibration.

Cytology: The branch of biology concerned with the study of cells.

Cytoplasm: The semifluid substance inside a cell that surrounds the nucleus and the other membrane-enclosed organelles.

D

Decanting: The process of separating a suspension by waiting for its heavier components to settle out and then pouring off the lighter ones.

experiment
CENTRAL

Decibel (dB): A unit of measurement for sound.

Deciduous: Plants that lose their leaves at some season of the year, and then grow them back at another season.

Decomposition: The breakdown of complex molecules—molecules of which dead organisms are composed—into simple nutrients that can be reutilized by living organisms.

Decomposition reaction: A chemical reaction in which one substance is broken down into two or more substances.

Denaturization: Altering of an enzyme so it no longer works.

Density: The mass of a substance compared to its volume.

Density ball: A ball with the fixed standard of 1.0 g/l, which is the exact density of pure water.

Dependent variable: The variable in a function whose value depends on the value of another variable in the function.

Deposition: Dropping of sediments that occurs when a river loses its energy of motion.

Desert: A biome with a hot-to-cool climate and dry weather.

Desertification: Transformation of arid or semiarid productive land into desert.

Dewpoint: The point at which water vapor begins to condense.

Dicot: Plants with a pair of embryonic seeds that appear at germination.

Diffraction: The bending of light or another form of electromagnetic radiation as it passes through a tiny hole or around a sharp edge.

Diffraction grating: A device consisting of a surface into which are etched very fine, closely spaced grooves that cause different wavelengths of light to reflect or refract (bend) by different amounts.

Diffusion: Random movement of molecules that leads to a net movement of molecules from a region of high concentration to a region of low concentration.

Disinfection: Using chemicals to kill harmful organisms.

Dissolved oxygen (DO): Oxygen molecules that have dissolved in water.

Distillation: The process of separating liquids from solids or from other liquids with different boiling points by a method of evaporation and condensation, so that each component in a mixture can be collected separately in its pure form.

DNA: Abbreviation for deoxyribonucleic acid. Large, complex molecules found in nuclei of cells that carry genetic information for an organism's development.

Domain: Small regions in an iron object that possess their own magnetic charges.

Dormancy: A state of inactivity in an organism.

Dormant: Describing an inactive organism.

Drought: A prolonged period of dry weather that damages crops or prevents their growth.

Dry cell: An electrolytic cell or battery using a non-liquid electrolyte.

Dynamic equilibrium: A situation in which substances are moving into and out of cell walls at an equal rate.

E

Earthquake: An unpredictable event in which masses of rock shift below Earth's surface, releasing enormous amounts of energy and sending out shock waves that sometimes cause the ground to shake dramatically.

Eclipse: A phenomenon in which the light from a celestial body is temporarily cut off by the presence of another body.

Ecologists: Scientists who study the interrelationship of organisms and their environments.

Ecosystem: An ecological community, including plants, animals and microorganisms considered together with their environment.

Electric charge repulsion: Repulsion of particles caused by a layer of negative ions surrounding each particle. The repulsion prevents coagulation and promotes the even dispersion of such particles through a mixture.

Electrical energy: The motion of electrons within any object that conducts electricity.

Electricity: A form of energy caused by the presence of electrical charges in matter.

Electrode: A material that will conduct an electrical current, usually a metal; used to carry electrons into or out of an electrochemical cell.

Electrolyte: Any substance that, when dissolved in water, conducts an electric current.

Electromagnetic spectrum: The complete array of electromagnetic radiation, including radio waves (at the longest-wavelength end), microwaves, infrared radiation, visible light, ultraviolet radiation, X rays, and gamma rays (at the shortest-wavelength end).

Electromagnetic waves: Radiation that has properties of both an electric and a magnetic wave and that travels through a vacuum at the speed of light.

Electromagnetism: A form of magnetic energy produced by the flow of an electric current through a metal core. Also, the study of electric and magnetic fields and their interaction with charges and currents.

Electron: A subatomic particle with a mass of about one atomic mass unit and a single electrical charge that orbits the nucleus of an atom.

Electroscope: A device that determines whether an object is electrically charged.

Elevation: Height above sea level.

Elliptical: An orbital path that is egg-shaped or resembles an elongated circle.

Embryo: The seed of a plant, which through germination can develop into a new plant; also, the earliest stage of animal development.

Embryonic: The earliest stages of development.

Endothermic reaction: A chemical reaction that absorbs energy, such as photosynthesis, the production of food by plant cells.

Energy: The ability to cause an action or for work to be done. Also, power that can be used to perform work, such as solar energy.

Environmental variables: Nonliving factors such as air temperature, water, pollution, and pH that can affect processes that occur in nature and in an experiment.

Enzymes: Any of numerous complex proteins produced by living cells that act as catalysts, speeding up the rate of chemical reactions in living organisms.

Enzymology: The science of studying enzymes.

Ephemerals: Plants that lie dormant in dry soil for years until major rainstorms occur.

Epicenter: The location where the seismic waves of an earthquake first appear on the surface, usually almost directly above the focus.

Equilibrium: A process in which the rates at which various changes take place balance each other, resulting in no overall change.

Erosion: The process by which topsoil is carried away by water, wind, or ice.

Eutrophic zone: The upper part of the ocean where sunlight penetrates, supporting plant life such as phytoplankton.

Eutrophication: Natural process by which a lake or other body of water becomes enriched in dissolved nutrients, spurring aquatic plant growth.

Evaporate/evaporation: The process by which liquid changes into a gas; also, the escape of water vapor into the air, yielding only the solute.

Exothermic reaction: A chemical reaction that releases energy, such as the burning of fuel.

Experiment: A controlled observation.

F

Fat: A type of lipid, or chemical compound used as a source of energy, to provide insulation, and to protect organs in an animal's body.

Fault: A crack running through rock that is the result of tectonic forces.

Fault blocks: Pieces of rock from Earth's crust that overlap and cause earthquakes when they press together and snap from pressure.

Filtration: The use of a screen or filter to separate larger particles from smaller ones that can slip through the filter's openings.

Fluorescence: Luminescence (glowing) that stops within 10 nanoseconds after an energy source has been removed.

Focal length: The distance of a focus from the surface of a lens or concave mirror.

Focal point: The point at which rays of light converge (come together) or from which they diverge (move apart).

Food web: An interconnected set of all the food chains in the same ecosystem.

Force: A physical interaction (pushing or pulling) tending to change the state of motion (velocity) of an object.

Fossil fuel: A fuel such as coal, oil, or natural gas that is formed over millions of years from the remains of plants and animals.

Fracture: A mineral's tendency to break into curved, rough, or jagged surfaces.

Frequency: The rate at which vibrations take place (number of times per second the motion is repeated), given in cycles per second or in hertz (Hz). Also, the number of waves that pass a given point in a given period of time.

Front: The front edges of moving masses of air.

Fungus: Kingdom of various single-celled or multicellular organisms, including mushrooms, molds, yeasts, and mildews, that do not contain chlorophyll. (Plural is fungi.)

Fusion: Combining of nuclei of two or more lighter elements into one nucleus of a heavier element; the process stars use to produce energy to support themselves against their own gravity.

G

Galaxy: A large collection of stars and clusters of stars containing anywhere from a few million to a few trillion stars.

Gene: A segment of a DNA (deoxyribonucleic acid) molecule contained in the nucleus of a cell that acts as a kind of code for the production of some specific protein. Genes carry instructions for the formation, functioning, and transmission of specific traits from one generation to another.

Genetic material: Material that transfers characteristics from a parent to its offspring.

Geology: The study of the origin, history, and structure of Earth.

Geotropism: The tendency of roots to bend toward Earth.

Germ theory of disease: The belief that disease is caused by germs.

Germination: The beginning of growth of a seed.

Gibbous moon: A phase of the Moon when more than half of its surface is lighted.

Glacier: A large mass of ice formed from snow that has packed together and which moves slowly down a slope under its own weight.

Global warming: Warming of Earth's atmosphere that results from an increase in the concentration of gases that store heat such as carbon dioxide.

Glucose: Also known as blood sugar; a simple sugar broken down in cells to produce energy.

Golgi body: Organelle that sorts, modifies, and packages molecules.

Gravity: Force of attraction between objects, the strength of which depends on the mass of each object and the distance between them.

Greenhouse effect: The warming of Earth's atmosphere due to water vapor, carbon dioxide, and other gases in the atmosphere that trap heat radiated from Earth's surface.

Greenhouse gases: Gases that absorb infrared radiation and warm air before it escapes into space.

Groundwater: Water that soaks into the ground and is stored in the small spaces between the rocks and soil.

H

Heat: A form of energy produced by the motion of molecules that make up a substance.

Heat energy: The energy produced when two substances that have different temperatures are combined.

Herbivore: Plant-eating organism.

experiment
CENTRAL

Hertz (Hz): The unit of frequency; a measure of the number of waves that pass a given point per second of time.

Heterotrophs: Organisms that cannot make their own food and that must, therefore, obtain their food from other organisms.

High air pressure: An area where the air molecules are more dense.

Hormone: A chemical produced in living cells that regulates the functions of the organism.

Humidity: The amount of water vapor (moisture) contained in the air.

Humus: Fragrant, spongy, nutrient-rich decayed plant or animal matter.

Hydrologic cycle: Continual movement of water from the atmosphere to Earth's surface through precipitation and back to the atmosphere through evaporation and transpiration.

Hydrologists: Scientists who study water and its cycle.

Hydrology: The study of water and its cycle.

Hydrometer: An instrument that determines the specific gravity of a liquid.

Hydrophilic: A substance that is attracted to and readily mixes with water.

Hydrophobic: A substance that is repelled by and does not mix with water.

Hydrotropism: The tendency of roots to grow toward a water source.

Hypertonic solution: A solution with a higher osmotic pressure (solute concentration) than another solution.

Hypothesis: An idea in the form of a statement that can be tested by observation and/or experiment.

Hypotonic solution: A solution with a lower osmotic pressure (solute concentration) than another solution.

words to know

I

Igneous rock: Rock formed from the cooling and hardening of magma.

Immiscible: Incapable of being mixed.

Impermeable: Not allowing substances to pass through.

Impurities: Chemicals or other pollutants in water.

Incomplete metamorphosis: Metamorphosis in which a nymph form gradually becomes an adult through molting.

Independent variable: The variable in a function that determines the final value of the function.

Indicator: Pigments that change color when they come into contact with acidic or basic solutions.

Inertia: The tendency of an object to continue in its state of motion.

Infrared radiation: Electromagnetic radiation of a wavelength shorter than radio waves but longer than visible light that takes the form of heat.

Inner core: Very dense, solid center of Earth.

Inorganic: Not made of or coming from living things.

Insulated wire: Electrical wire coated with a nonconducting material such as plastic.

Insulation/insulator: A material that does not conduct heat or electricity.

Interference fringes: Bands of color that fan around an object.

Ion: An atom or group of atoms that carries an electrical charge—either positive or negative—as a result of losing or gaining one or more electrons.

Ionic conduction: The flow of an electrical current by the movement of charged particles, or ions.

Isobars: Continuous lines on a map that connect areas with the same air pressure.

Isotonic solutions: Two solutions that have the same concentration of solute particles and therefore the same osmotic pressure.

K

Kinetic energy: Energy of an object or system due to its motion.

L

Lactobacilli: A strain of bacteria.

Larva: Immature form (wormlike in insects; fishlike in amphibians) of an organism capable of surviving on its own. A larva does not resemble the parent and must go through metamorphosis, or change, to reach its adult stage.

Lava: Molten rock that occurs at the surface of Earth, usually through volcanic eruptions.

Lens: A piece of transparent material with two curved surfaces that bring together and focus rays of light passing through it.

Lichen: An organism composed of a fungus and a photosynthetic organism in a symbiotic relationship.

Lift: Upper force on the wings of an aircraft created by differences in air pressure on top of and underneath the wings.

Light-year: Distance light travels in one year in the vacuum of space, roughly 5.9 trillion miles (9.5 trillion km).

The Local Group: A cluster of 30 galaxies, including the Milky Way, pulled together gravitationally.

Low air pressure: An area where the air molecules are less dense.

Lunar eclipse: Eclipse that occurs when Earth passes between the Sun and the Moon, casting a shadow on the Moon.

Luster: A glow of reflected light; a sheen.

M

Macroorganisms: Visible organisms that aid in breaking down organic matter.

Magma: Molten rock deep within Earth that consists of liquids, gases, and particles of rocks and crystals. Magma underlies areas of volcanic activity and at Earth's surface is called lava.

Magma chambers: Pools of bubbling liquid rock that are the energy sources causing volcanoes to be active.

Magma surge: A swell or rising wave of magma caused by the movement and friction of tectonic plates; the surge heats and melts rock, adding to the magma and its force.

Magnet: A material that attracts other like material, especially metals.

Magnetic circuit: A series of magnetic domains aligned in the same direction.

Magnetic field: The space around an electric current or a magnet in which a magnetic force can be observed.

Magnetism: A fundamental force of nature caused by the motion of electrons in an atom. Magnetism is manifested by the attraction of certain materials for iron.

Mantle: Thick, dense layer of rock that underlies Earth's crust and overlies the core.

Manure: The waste matter of animals.

Mass: Measure of the total amount of matter in an object. Also, an object's quantity of matter as shown by its gravitational pull on another object.

Matter: Anything that has mass and takes up space.

Meandering river: A lowland river that twists and turns along its route to the sea.

Medium: A material that carries the acoustic vibrations away from the body producing them.

Meniscus: The curved surface of a column of liquid.

Metamorphic rock: Rock formed by transformation of pre-existing rock through changes in temperature and pressure.

Metamorphosis: Transformation of an immature animal into an adult.

Meteorologists: Scientists who study weather and weather forecasting.

Microbiology: Branch of biology dealing with microscopic forms of life.

Microclimate: A local climate.

Microorganisms: Living organisms so small that they can be seen only with the aid of a microscope.

Micropyle: Seed opening that enables water to enter easily.

Milky Way: The galaxy in which our solar system is located.

Mineral: An inorganic substance found in nature with a definite chemical composition and structure. As a nutrient, helps build bones and soft tissues and regulates body functions.

Mixtures: Combinations of two or more substances that are not chemically combined with each other and can exist in any proportion.

Molecule: The smallest particle of a substance that retains all the properties of the substance and is composed of one or more atoms.

Molting: Shedding of the outer layer of an animal, as occurs during growth of insect larvae.

Monocot: Plants with a single embryonic seed at germination.

Moraine: Mass of boulders, stones, and other rock debris carried along and deposited by a glacier.

Multicellular: Living things with many cells joined together.

N

Nanometer: A unit of length; this measurement is equal to one-billionth of a meter.

Nansen bottles: Self-closing containers with thermometers that draw in water at different depths.

Nebula: Bright or dark cloud, often composed of gases and dust, hovering in the space between the stars.

Neutralization: A chemical process in which the mixing of an acidic solution with a basic (alkaline) solution results in a solution that has the properties of neither an acid nor a base.

Neutron: A subatomic particle with a mass of about one atomic mass unit and no electrical charge that is found in the nucleus of an atom.

Niche: The specific role that an organism carries out in its ecosystem.

Nonpoint source: An unidentified source of pollution; may actually be a number of sources.

Nucleus: The central core of an atom, consisting of protons and (usually) neutrons.

Nutrient: A substance needed by an organism in order for it to survive, grow, and develop.

Nutrition: The study of the food nutrients an organism needs in order to maintain well-being.

Nymph: An immature form in the life cycle of insects that go through an incomplete metamorphosis.

o

Oceanography: The study of the chemistry of the oceans, as well as their currents, marine life, and the ocean bed.

Optics: The study of the nature of light and its properties.

Organelles: Membrane-bounded cellular "organs" performing a specific set of functions within a eukaryotic cell.

Organic: Made of or coming from living things.

Osmosis: The movement of fluids and substances dissolved in liquids across a semipermeable membrane from an area of its greater concentration to an area of its lesser concentration until all substances involved reach a balance.

Outer core: A liquid core that surrounds Earth's solid inner core; made mostly of iron.

Oxidation: A chemical reaction in which oxygen reacts with some other substance and in which ions, atoms, or molecules lose electrons.

Oxidation-reduction reaction: A chemical reaction in which one substance loses one or more electrons and the other substance gains one or more electrons.

Oxidation state: The sum of an atom's positive and negative charges.

Oxidizing agent: A chemical substance that gives up oxygen or takes on electrons from another substance.

Ozone layer: The atmospheric layer of approximately 15 to 30 miles (24 to 48 km) above Earth's surface in which the concentration of ozone is significantly higher than in other parts of the atmosphere and that protects the lower atmosphere from harmful solar radiation.

P

Papain: An enzyme obtained from the fruit of the papaya used as a meat tenderizer, as a drug to clean cuts and wounds, and as a digestive aid for stomach disorders.

Passive solar energy system: A solar energy system in which the heat of the Sun is captured, used, and stored by means of the design of a building and the materials from which it is made.

Pasteurization: The process of slow heating that kills bacteria and other microorganisms.

Penicillin: A mold from the fungi group of microorganisms used as an antibiotic.

Pepsin: Digestive enzyme that breaks down protein.

Percolate: To pass through a permeable substance.

Permeable: Having pores that permit a liquid or a gas to pass through.

pH: Abbreviation for potential hydrogen. A measure of the acidity or alkalinity of a solution determined by the concentration of hydrogen ions present in a liter of a given fluid. The pH scale ranges from 0 (greatest concentration of hydrogen ions and therefore most acidic) to 14 (least concentration of hydrogen ions and therefore most alkaline), with 7 representing a neutral solution, such as pure water.

Pharmacology: The science dealing with the properties, reactions, and therapeutic values of drugs.

Phases: Changes in the illuminated Moon surfaces as the Moon revolves around Earth.

Phloem: Plant tissue consisting of elongated cells that transport carbohydrates and other nutrients.

Phosphorescence: Luminescence (glowing) that stops within 10 nanoseconds after an energy source has been removed.

Photoelectric effect: The phenomenon in which light falling upon certain metals stimulates the emission of electrons and changes light into electricity.

Photosynthesis: Chemical process by which plants containing chlorophyll use sunlight to manufacture their own food by converting carbon dioxide and water to carbohydrates, releasing oxygen as a by-product.

Phototropism: The tendency of a plant to grow toward a source of light.

Photovoltaic cells: A device made of silicon that converts sunlight into electricity.

Physical change: A change in which the substance keeps its identity, such as a piece of chalk that has been ground up.

Physical property: A characteristic that you can detect with your senses, such as color and shape.

Phytoplankton: Microscopic aquatic plants that live suspended in the water.

Pigment: A substance that displays a color because of the wavelengths of light that it reflects.

Pitch: A property of a sound, determined by its frequency; the highness or lowness of a sound.

Plates: Large regions of Earth's surface, composed of the crust and uppermost mantle, which move about, forming many of Earth's major geologic surface features.

Pnematocysts: Stinging cells.

Point source: An identified source of pollution.

Pollination: The transfer of pollen from the male reproductive organs to the female reproductive organs of plants.

Pore: An opening or space.

Potential energy: The energy possessed by a body as a result of its position.

Precipitation: Water in its liquid or frozen form when it falls from clouds as rain, snow, sleet, or hail.

Probe: The terminal of a voltmeter, used to connect the voltmeter to a circuit.

Producer: An organism that can manufacture its own food from nonliving materials and an external energy source, usually by photosynthesis.

Product: A compound that is formed as a result of a chemical reaction.

Prominences: Masses of glowing gas, mainly hydrogen, that rise from the Sun's surface like flames.

Propeller: Radiating blades mounted on a quickly rotating shaft that are used to move aircraft forward.

Protein: A complex chemical compound that consists of many amino acids attached to each other that are essential to the structure and functioning of all living cells.

Protists: Members of the kingdom Protista, primarily single-celled organisms that are not plants or animals.

Proton: A subatomic particle with a mass of about one atomic mass unit and a single negative electrical change that is found in the nucleus of an atom.

Protozoan: Single-celled animal-like microscopic organisms that live by taking in food rather than making it by photosynthesis and must live in the presence of water. (Plural is protozoa.)

Pupa: A stage in the metamorphosis of an insect during which its tissues are completely reorganized to take on their adult shape.

R

Radiation: Energy transmitted in the form of electromagnetic waves or subatomic particles.

Radicule: A seed's root system.

Radio wave: Longest form of electromagnetic radiation, measuring up to 6 miles (9.6 km) from peak to peak.

Radiosonde balloons: Instruments for collecting data in the atmosphere and then transmitting that data back to Earth by means of radio waves.

Reactant: A compound present at the beginning of a chemical reaction.

Reaction: Response to an action prompted by a stimulus.

Reduction: A process in which a chemical substance gives off oxygen or takes on electrons.

Reflection: The bouncing of light rays in a regular pattern off the surface of an object.

Refraction: The bending of light rays as they pass at an angle from one transparent or clear medium into a second one of different density.

Rennin: Enzyme used in making cheese.

Resistance: A partial or complete limiting of the flow of electrical current through a material.

Respiration: The physical process that supplies oxygen to living cells and the chemical reactions that take place inside the cells.

Resultant: A force that results from the combined action of two other forces.

Retina: The light-sensitive part of the eyeball that receives images and transmits visual impulses through the optic nerve to the brain.

River: A main course of water into which many other smaller bodies of water flow.

Rock: Naturally occurring solid mixture of minerals.

Runoff: Water in excess of what can be absorbed by the ground.

S

Salinity: The amount of salts dissolved in seawater.

Saturated: Containing the maximum amount of a solute for a given amount of solvent at a certain temperature.

Scientific method: Collecting evidence meticulously and then theorizing from it.

Scribes: Ancient scholars.

Scurvy: A disease caused by a deficiency of vitamin C, which causes a weakening of connective tissue in bone and muscle.

Sediment: Sand, silt, clay, rock, gravel, mud, or other matter that has been transported by flowing water.

Sedimentary rock: Rock formed from the compressed and solidified layers of organic or inorganic matter.

experiment
CENTRAL

Sedimentation: A process during which gravity pulls particles out of a liquid.

Seismic belt: Boundaries where Earth's plates meet.

Seismic waves: Classified as body waves or surface waves, vibrations in rock and soil that transfer the force of the earthquake from the focus (center) into the surrounding area.

Seismograph: A device that records vibrations of the ground and within Earth.

Seismology: The study and measurement of earthquakes.

Seismometer: A seismograph that measures the movement of the ground.

Semipermeable membrane: A thin barrier between two solutions that permits only certain components of the solutions, usually the solvent, to pass through.

Sexual reproduction: A reproductive process that involves the union of two individuals in the exchange of genetic material.

Silt: Medium-sized soil particles.

Solar collector: A device that absorbs sunlight and collects solar heat.

Solar eclipse: Eclipse that occurs when the Moon passes between Earth and the Sun, casting a shadow on Earth.

Solar energy: Any form of electromagnetic radiation that is emitted by the Sun.

Solute: The substance that is dissolved to make a solution and exists in the least amount in a solution, for example sugar in sugar water.

Solution: A mixture of two or more substances that appears to be uniform throughout except on a molecular level.

Solvent: The major component of a solution or the liquid in which some other component is dissolved, for example water in sugar water.

Specific gravity: The ratio of the density of a substance to the density of another substance.

Spectrum: Range of individual wavelengths of radiation produced when white light is broken down into its component colors when it passes through a prism or is broken apart by some other means.

Standard: A base for comparison.

Star: A vast clump of hydrogen gas and dust that produces great energy through fusion reactions at its core.

Static electricity: A form of electricity produced by friction in which the electric charge does not flow in a current but stays in one place.

Streak: The color of the dust left when a mineral is rubbed across a surface.

Substrate: The substance on which an enzyme operates in a chemical reaction.

Succulent: Plants that live in dry environments and have water storage tissue.

Surface water: Water in lakes, rivers, ponds, and streams.

Suspension: A temporary mixture of a solid in a gas or liquid from which the solid will eventually settle out.

Symbiosis: A pattern in which two or more organisms live in close connection with each other, often to the benefit of both or all organisms.

Synthesis reaction: A chemical reaction in which two or more substances combine to form a new substance.

T

Taiga: A large land biome mostly dominated by coniferous trees.

Tectonic plates: Huge flat rocks that form Earth's crust.

Temperate: Mild or moderate weather conditions.

Temperature: The measure of the average energy of the molecules in a substance.

Terminal: A connection in an electric circuit; usually a connection on a source of electric energy such as a battery.

Terracing: A series of horizontal ridges made in a hillside to reduce erosion.

Testa: A tough outer layer that protects the embryo and endosperm of a seed from damage.

Thermal conductivity: A number representing a material's ability to conduct heat.

Thermal energy: Energy caused by the movement of molecules due to the transfer of heat.

Thiamine: A vitamin of the B complex that is essential to normal metabolism and nerve function.

Thigmotropism: The tendency for a plant to grow toward a surface it touches.

Titration: A procedure in which an acid and a base are slowly mixed to achieve a neutral substance.

Toxic: Poisonous.

Trace element: A chemical element present in minute quantities.

Translucent: Permits the passage of light.

Tropism: The growth or movement of a plant toward or away from a stimulus.

Troposphere: The lowest layer of Earth's atmosphere, ranging to an altitude of about 9 miles (15 km) above Earth's surface.

Tsunami: A tidal wave caused by an earthquake.

Tuber: An underground, starch-storing stem, such as a potato.

Tundra: A treeless, frozen biome with low-lying plants.

Turbulence: Air disturbance or unrest that affects an aircraft's flight.

Tyndall effect: The effect achieved when colloidal particles reflect a beam of light, making it visible when shined through such a mixture.

U

Ultraviolet: Electromagnetic radiation (energy) of a wavelength just shorter than the violet (shortest wavelength) end of the visible light spectrum and thus with higher energy than the visible light.

Unconfined aquifer: An aquifer under a layer of permeable rock and soil.

Unicellular: Living things that have one cell. Protozoans are unicellular.

Universal gravitation: The notion of the constancy of the force of gravity between two bodies.

V

Vacuole: A space-filling organelle of plant cells.

Variable: Something that can change the results of an experiment.

Vegetative propagation: A form of asexual reproduction in which plants are produced that are genetically identical to the parent.

Viable: The capability of developing or growing under favorable conditions.

Vibration: A regular, back-and-forth motion of molecules in the air.

Visible spectrum: Light waves visible to the eye.

Vitamin: A complex organic compound found naturally in plants and animals that the body needs in small amounts for normal growth and activity.

Volcano: A conical mountain or dome of lava, ash, and cinders that forms around a vent leading to molten rock deep within Earth.

Voltage: Also called potential difference; the amount of electric energy stored in a mass of electric charges compared to the energy stored in some other mass of charges.

Voltmeter: An instrument for measuring the conductivity or resistance in a circuit or the voltage produced by an electric source.

Volume: The amount of space occupied by a three-dimensional object; the amplitude or loudness of a sound.

W

Water (hydrologic) cycle: The constant movement of water molecules on Earth as they rise into the atmosphere as water vapor, condense into droplets and fall to land or bodies of water, evaporate, and rise again.

Waterline: The highest point to which water rises on the hull of a ship. The portion of the hull below the waterline is under water.

Water table: The upper surface of groundwater.

Water vapor: Water in its gaseous state.

Wave: A motion in which energy and momentum is carried away from some source.

Wavelength: The distance between the peak of a wave of light, heat, or energy and the next corresponding peak.

Weather: The state of the troposphere at a particular time and place.

Weather forecasting: The scientific predictions of future weather patterns.

Weight: The gravitational attraction of Earth on an object; the measure of the heaviness of an object.

Wetlands: Areas that are wet or covered with water for at least part of the year.

X

Xanthophyll: Yellow pigment in plants.

Xerophytes: Plants that require little water to survive.

Xylem: Plant tissue consisting of elongated, thick-walled cells that transport water and mineral nutrients.

experiment
CENTRAL

chapter 25

Magnetism

One of the most mysterious phenomena we witness every day is **magnetism,** a fundamental force of nature caused by the motion of electrons in an atom. You put a note on a refrigerator door. You watch the speedometer in a car tell you how fast you are travelling. You listen to a tape of recorded music. All of these depend on magnetism, but how do these things work? How does the simple physics of the magnet make so much possible?

Magnetism is a matter of alignment

What turns an ordinary piece of iron into a magnet? A large iron bar actually contains millions of "mini-magnets," small magnetized areas called **domains.** Each has a north pole and a south pole. If the poles of the iron's domains are aimed in all different directions, their magnetic forces act against one another and cancel each other out. When all of the domains are facing the same way, the bar becomes a magnet because it now has a single, strong **magnetic field,** a space in which its magnetic force can be observed.

How can we get all the domains facing the same way? This can be achieved by repeatedly rubbing the bar with one pole of another magnet in the same direction. Once the bar is magnetized, its magnetic field will exert enough force on the domains in nearby iron filings to temporarily magnetize them. Each filing has its own north and south poles, and those poles are attracted to or repelled by the magnet's poles. (Remember that unlike poles attract and like poles repel.)

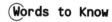

Words to Know

Alignment:
Adjustment in a certain direction or orientation.

Alloy:
A mixture of two or more metals with properties different from those metals of which it is made.

Circuit:
The complete path of an electric current including the source of electric energy.

Control experiment:
A setup that is identical to the experiment but is not affected by the variable that affects the experimental group.

experiment
CENTRAL

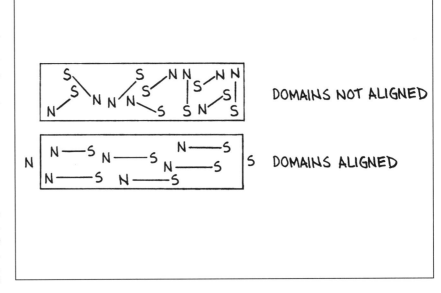

DOMAINS NOT ALIGNED

DOMAINS ALIGNED

The position of the domains in such a magnet is not permanent, however. Striking or jarring the bar will literally knock its domains out of **alignment**, and the bar will lose its magnetism. Even as time passes and the magnet sits in a drawer, it will slowly lose its magnetism as the domains shift back to their original positions. One way to preserve a

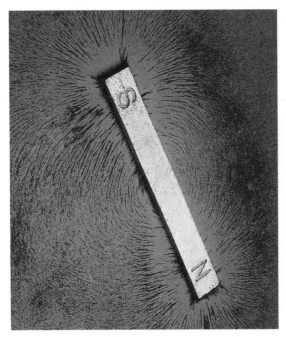

magnet is to keep it in a **magnetic circuit**, in which each domain is held in place by the direction of the next domain. Placing a steel plate across the poles of a horseshoe magnet will complete the circuit: all the domains in the circuit will point in the same direction and will tend to remain that way.

In the first experiment you will create a magnet and then test the effects on the magnet's strength of heat, cold, jarring, and rubbing with another magnet.

The "keeper" placed across the positive and negative poles of this horseshoe magnet creates a magnetic circuit that holds the domains in place and stops the magnet from losing its strength.

Electricity can also produce magnetism

Electrical current flowing through a wire produces a magnetic field. If the wire is wound into a coil, it will produce a stronger magnetic field, similar to that of a bar magnet: each end of the coil will become a magnetic pole. This effect was discovered by Danish physicist Hans Christian Oersted (1777–1851). He noticed that electric current disturbed the normal functioning of magnetic compasses.

Electromagnetism is a form of magnetic energy produced by the flow of an electric current through a metal core. It has many applications in our modern technology. Stereo speakers are one of the most common applications. Electrical signals pass through a coil, creating a varying magnetic field that pushes and pulls on another magnet attached to the speaker. This causes the paper speaker cone to move back and forth to produce sound. Some metals, including iron, can be made into electromagnets strong enough to lift tons of scrap steel. One advantage of electromagnets is that they can be turned on and off with the flip of a switch.

In the second experiment, you will create a small electromagnet using an electric current and you will test the effect on the magnet when the strength of the current is varied.

⒲**ords to Know**

Domain:
Small regions in iron that possess their own magnetic charges.

Electron:
A subatomic particle with a mass of about one atomic mass unit and a single electrical charge that orbits the nucleus of an atom.

Electromagnetism:
A form of magnetic energy produced by the flow of an electric current through a metal core. Also, the study of electric and magnetic fields and their interaction with charges and currents.

Hypothesis:
An idea in the form of a statement that can be tested by observation and/or experiment.

Insulated wire:
Electrical wire coated with a non-conducting material such as plastic.

The electromagnet is especially useful in the scrap yard because it can be easily switched on and off. (Photo Researchers Inc. Reproduced by permission.)

ⓌWords to Know

Magnetic circuit:
A series of magnetic domains aligned in the same direction.

Magnetic field:
The space around an electric current or a magnet in which a magnetic force can be observed.

Magnetism:
A fundamental force in nature caused by the motion of electrons in an atom.

Terminal:
A connection in an electric circuit; usually a connection on a source of electric energy such as a battery.

Variable:
Something that can affect the results of an experiment.

experiment
CENTRAL

Experiment 1

Magnets: How do heat, cold, jarring, and rubbing affect the magnetism of a nail?

Purpose/Hypothesis

In this experiment, you will first test the effect of rubbing a bar magnet on a steel or iron nail. The bar magnet should align the domains in the iron so that the nail becomes magnetized. You will then measure the effect of four actions upon the nail's magnetic strength—heating, cooling, rubbing with a magnet in the opposite direction, and striking with a hammer. Each of the four actions will be tested on a different magnetized nail. Before you begin, make an educated guess about the outcome of this experiment based on your knowledge of magnetism. This educated guess, or prediction, is your **hypothesis.** A hypothesis should explain these things:

 ## What Are the Variables?

Variables are anything that might affect the results of an experiment. Here are the main variables in this experiment:

- type of metal in the nails

- the size of the nails

- the strength of the bar magnet used

- the number of times the nail is rubbed with the bar magnet

- the direction in which the nail is rubbed with the bar magnet

- the actions performed on the nails (striking, heating, etc.)

   In other words, the variables in this experiment are anything that might affect the magnetic strength of the nails. If you change more than one variable for each nail, you will not be able to tell which variable had the most effect on the resulting magnetic strength of the nail.

- the topic of the experiment
- the variable you will change
- the variable you will measure
- what you expect to happen

A hypothesis should be brief, specific, and measurable. It must be something you can test through observation. Your experiment will prove or disprove whether your hypothesis is correct. Here is one possible hypothesis for this experiment: "Rubbing a magnetized nail with the opposite pole of the bar magnet that was used to magnetize it, striking or dropping it, and raising or lowering its temperature will decrease the strength of its magnetic field."

In this case, the **variables** you will change are the four actions you will take on identically magnetized nails, and the variable you will measure is the resulting strength of the nail's magnetic field. You expect that all four actions will reduce the nail's magnetic strength.

A fifth nail will be magnetized and tested without any action performed on it. This **control experiment** lets us know that any changes we see in magnetism result from the actions and not from some unseen factor.

Level of Difficulty
Easy/moderate.

Materials Needed
- bar magnet
- 5 steel or iron nails about 3 inches (7.5 centimeters) long (iron is preferable; steel is an **alloy** containing other metals that cannot be magnetized)
- hammer
- 1 cup of hot tap water
- 1 cup of cold tap water with ice added
- 10 staples (separated and unused)
- 10 steel paper clips
- 10 plastic-coated paper clips
- small wooden block
- safety glasses

Approximate Budget
Less than $10 for the magnet. (Try to borrow the hammer and safety glasses, if you do not have them.)

How to Experiment Safely

Safety glasses must be worn any time you are striking metal on metal. Do not strike the nail with great force, and be sure to rest the nail on the wooden block so it does not bend or snap when hit. Do not lift the hammer more than 6 inches (15 centimeters) from the block. (See illustration below.)

Timetable

About 30 minutes.

Step-by-Step Instructions

1. Rub one pole of the bar magnet lengthwise down one nail fifty times, always in the same direction.

2. Test the nail for magnetism by touching its point to a staple, then to a steel paper clip, then to a coated paper clip.

3. Observe and record on your data chart which objects the nail can lift. Carefully set the nail aside. Keep it several inches away from the other nails.

Rest the shaft of the nail flat on the block.

	Trial #1			Action
	staples	paper clips	coated paper clips	
NAIL #1				hot
NAIL #2				cold
NAIL #3				rubbing
NAIL #4				jarring
NAIL #5				(control)

Step 4: Data chart for Experiment 1.

4. Repeat this procedure with three other nails, rubbing them the same number of times in the same direction with the same pole of the bar magnet. The magnetic strength of the nails should be almost the same. If one is significantly weaker, rub it with the magnet until the strength of its field is similar to the others. Your data chart should look like the illustration.

5. To establish your control experiment, test the remaining nail for magnetism. If this nail picks up any of the test objects, it has somehow been magnetized. Do not be surprised if the nail does have a very weak magnetic field. Just the movements of nails against one another in a box can align a small percentage of the domains in the metal. To prove that rubbing the first four nails with the bar magnet caused them to become magnetized, however, you must see a significant difference between their magnetic strength and that of the control nail.

experiment
CENTRAL

6. Now rub the control nail the same number of times in the same direction. Check to be sure it is magnetized, record the results, and carefully set it aside away from the other nails.

7. Perform one action on each nail. (Remember not to disturb the control nail.)

a. Place the first nail in hot water and leave it for ten minutes.

b. Place the second nail in the ice water and leave it for ten minutes.

c. Rub the third nail with the same pole of the magnet used earlier, but in the opposite direction, twenty-five times.

d. With everyone present wearing safety goggles, place the shaft of the fourth nail flat on the wooden block and strike it firmly three or four times. (Do not lift the head of the hammer any more than 6 inches [15 centimeters].)

8. Test the magnetic strength of each nail and note any changes on your chart.

9. Finally, check the control nail to make sure that nails do not lose their magnetic strength simply by sitting unused for several minutes. Record the strength of the control nail in the appropriate row on your chart.

Summary of Results

Compare your data from the four tests. Determine which of the actions demagnetized the nails and which did not. Check your findings against the predictions you made in your hypothesis. Which actions did you accurately predict would demagnetize the nails? Which actions did not have the effect you expected? Summarize your results in writing.

Change the Variables

By altering your variables, you can make this experiment the basis of a series of interesting and informative investigations into magnetism. For example, how fast does magnetic strength weaken? Can we preserve a magnet longer by refrigerating it? Are the effects of demagnetization always reversible, or can domains be put permanently out of order?

Troubleshooter's Guide

This experiment is fairly straightforward. You should encounter little difficulty if you use the listed materials. When you are doing experiments with magnetism, results can be difficult to measure precisely. To compare the strengths of magnets, test their lifting power several times and average the results to achieve a greater degree of accuracy.

Here are some problems that may arise during the experiment, some possible causes, and ways to remedy the problems.

Problem: All of the nails are strongly magnetized to start with.

Possible cause: They may have been exposed to a strong magnetic field prior to the experiment. Demagnetize them by striking each several times with the hammer. (It is not necessary to strike with great force. Remember to wear safety glasses and place the nails flat on a wooden block so they will not bend or snap.)

Problem: The nails will not magnetize.

Possible causes:

1. The nails are made of a metal or alloy that cannot be magnetized. Use iron or steel nails. (Iron is preferable.)

2. Your bar magnet is too weak. Check its strength and replace it if necessary.

3. You are changing the direction of the stroke as you rub the magnet on the nail, or you are accidentally switching poles as you rub the nail. Either mistake will sweep the nail's domains in different directions. Follow this procedure carefully.

Experiment 2
Electromagnets: Does the strength of an electromagnet increase with greater current?

Purpose/Hypothesis

In this experiment, you will create an electromagnet and test the effect of varying levels of electric current on the strength of the magnetic field. You will increase the current by adding batteries to the **circuit**—the path of the electric current through a wire attached to the **terminals** of a source of electric energy. Before you begin, make an educated guess about the outcome of this experiment based on your knowledge of electromagnets. This educated guess, or prediction, is your **hypothesis.** A hypothesis should explain these things:

- the topic of the experiment
- the variable you will change
- the variable you will measure
- what you expect to happen

A hypothesis should be brief, specific, and measurable. It must be something you can test through observation. Your experiment will

What Are the Variables?

Variables are anything that might affect the results of an experiment. Here are the main variables in this experiment:

- the type of nail used

- the number of batteries attached to the circuit, which is directly proportional to the current

- the type and gauge of wire used

- the shape and weight of the test objects used

   In other words, the variables in this experiment are everything that might affect the magnetic field strength of the electromagnet. If you change more than one variable, you will not be able to tell which variable had the most effect on the magnetic strength.

prove or disprove whether your hypothesis is correct. Here is one possible hypothesis for this experiment: "The strength of an electromagnet's magnetic field will increase when the current applied to the electromagnet is increased."

In this case, the **variable** you will change is the electrical current, and the variable you will measure is the resulting strength of the magnetic field of the electromagnet. You expect that a higher current will result in a higher magnetic field strength.

Level of Difficulty
Easy/moderate.

Materials Needed
- 2 feet (.6 meter) of insulated, 16 to 18 gauge solid copper wire
- 3 fresh D-cell batteries
- iron or steel nail (iron is preferable)
- electrical tape
- 10 staples (separated and unused)
- 10 steel paper clips
- 10 plastic-coated paper clips
- magnetic compass
- wire strippers

Approximate Budget
Less than $15 for wire, batteries, and electrical tape. (Try to borrow the wire strippers and compass, if necessary.)

Timetable
15 to 20 minutes.

Step-by-Step Instructions
1. Secure one of the D-cell batteries to a flat surface using a strip of electrical tape.

2. Coil the insulated copper wire ten or more times around the nail, starting at one end of the nail and working toward the other. Leave about 2 inches (5 centimeters) of straight wire at each end.

3. Strip the insulation off both ends of the wire. Hold one end to the positive terminal on the battery, and the other end to the negative terminal.

4. Check the nail for a magnetic field by holding it over the compass. Does the compass needle always point along the same direction on the nail? Which end of the coil forms the north pole of the magnetic field, the one leading to the positive terminal or the one leading to the negative terminal?

5. Use the magnet to lift as many staples as possible. Repeat with the steel paper clips and with the coated paper clips.

6. Record on your data chart the number lifted each time. Your chart should look like the illustration on page 382.

7. Increase the voltage applied to the electromagnet by adding another D-cell battery to the circuit. This will double the electrical current. Secure the batteries firmly together with electrical tape, making sure the positive terminal of one is touching the negative terminal of the other.

8. Repeat the test of the magnet's lifting power and record your observations on the chart.

9. Finally, repeat the tests once more with three batter-

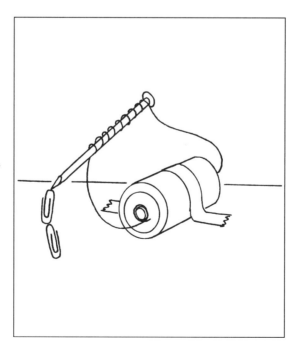

Steps 1 to 3: Set-up of nail and D-cell battery.

	Strength (no. lifted)		
	staples	steel paper clips	coated paper clips
1.5v	4	1	0
3.0v	7	3	0
4.5v			

Voltage (vertical axis label on left)

Step 6: Sample data chart for Experiment 2.

ies. This will triple the current. Do not use more than three D-cell batteries! Do not use any other type of battery without first asking your teacher.

Summary of Results

Your data from Steps 6, 8, and 9 should be recorded on a chart. This chart should contain the information that will show whether your hypothesis is correct. Did changes in current strength affect the magnetic strength? You can increase the clarity of your results by converting the data into graph form. Summarize your results in writing.

Change the Variables

To further explore the topic of electromagnetism, you can vary this experiment in the following ways:

- Use a different type of nail, such as copper or aluminum, or a heavier iron or steel nail
- Try a heavier gauge copper wire
- Vary the shape and weight of the items you try to pick up

One variation you must avoid is adding more than three batteries to the circuit or using a kind of battery other than D-cell. This can create enough electric current to be dangerous.

Troubleshooter's Guide

When doing experiments with magnetism, results can be difficult to measure precisely. To compare the strengths of magnets, test their lifting power several times and average the results to achieve a greater degree of accuracy.

Here is a problem that may arise during the experiment, some possible causes, and ways to remedy the problems.

Problem: The nail does not show any magnetism.

Possible causes:

1. A connection is loose. Check your connections, especially where the copper wire meets the battery terminals. Secure them with electrical tape if necessary.

2. The nail is made of a metal or alloy that does not magnetize. Use an iron nail.

3. You are using uninsulated wire, causing the current to travel across the coil and disrupt the magnetic field. Use **insulated wire.**

4. Your batteries are dead. Check them with a flashlight and replace them if necessary.

Design Your Own Experiment

How to Select a Topic Relating to this Concept

If you look carefully around your house, you will discover that magnets play a hidden role in much of the technology we use today. You can investigate other uses of magnets and develop interesting ideas for experiments and demonstrations. Remember that magnetic particles make tape recordings and computer diskettes function. Magnets are at work in every electric motor you see. Magnetism also affects natural phenomena, such as the aurora borealis (northern lights) and the migratory patterns of birds.

experiment
CENTRAL

Check the For More Information section and talk with your science teacher of school or community media specialist to start gathering information on magnetism questions that interest you. Remember that any experiment involving electricity should use no more than three 1.5-volt batteries, and any experiment proposal should be approved by your teacher.

Steps in the Scientific Method

To do an original experiment, you need to plan carefully and think things through. Otherwise, you might not be sure what question you are answering, what you are or should be measuring, or what your findings prove or disprove.

Here are the steps in designing an experiment:

- State the purpose of—and the underlying question behind—the experiment you propose to do.
- Recognize the variables involved, and select one that will help you answer the question at hand.
- State your hypothesis, an educated guess about the answer to your question.
- Decide how to change the variable you have selected.
- Decide how to measure your results.

Recording Data and Summarizing the Results

In the experiments included here, and in any experiments you develop, try to display your data in accurate and interesting ways. When presenting your results to those who have not seen the experiment performed, showing photographs of the various steps can make the process more interesting and clear.

Related Projects

Simple variations on the two experiments in this section can prove valuable and informative. The magnetic field created by an electromagnet has poles just like a permanent magnet. How could you discover which end of the coil is north and which is south? How does reversing the positive and negative contacts on the coil affect the field? What happens if you put an electromagnet coil around an already magnetized nail? Does it increase the strength of the field?

For More Information

Gillett, Kate, ed. *The Knowledge Factory.* Brookfield, CT: Copper Beech Books, 1996. ❖ Provides some fun and enlightening observations on questions relevant to this topic, along with good ideas for projects and demonstrations.

Kent, Amanda, and Alan Ward. *Introduction to Physics.* London: Usborne Publishing, Ltd., 1983. ❖ Includes detailed, easily comprehensible illustrations and explanations of applications of magnetism in everyday life.

Ray, C. Claibourne. *The New York Times Book of Science Questions and Answers.* New York: Doubleday, 1997. ❖ Addresses both everyday observations and advanced scientific concepts on a wide variety of subjects.

chapter 26

Microorganisms

In 1675, Anton van Leeuwenhoek (1632–1723), a Dutch merchant with an interest in science, looked through a microscope at a drop of stagnant water. He had originally built a simple microscope to examine textile threads for the draperies he made. Eventually, as a result of his scientific investigations, he built a more powerful microscope that could magnify objects 200 times. Under such a microscope, van Leeuwenhoek saw that the dirty water was full of tiny living creatures. Before his discovery, the smallest living creatures known were tiny insects. He called the life forms he looked at **animalcules,** but they would later become known as **protozoa** and **bacteria.** Other scientists would also find different life forms under the microscope and give them specific names. In time, the term **microorganisms** would be used to describe all microscopic forms of life.

Connecting bacteria to disease

Van Leeuwenhoek's animalcules had an active life, scurrying around by means of small whip-like tails or by expelling streams of fluid. The bacteria he observed were quieter. They mostly lay about and multiplied. It was Louis Pasteur (1822–1895), a French chemist, who pieced together the connection between disease and these microorganisms.

In the 1850s, while Pasteur was a professor and dean at the University of Lille in France, he helped a man who wanted to know why some of his sugar-beet juice, which was being distilled for alcohol, was going bad. What Pasteur discovered were rodlike organisms in the bad batches. They were bacteria, which multiply quickly. In his experiment, he found that heat killed these microorganisms.

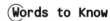

Words to Know

Animalcules:
Life forms that Anton van Leeuwenhoek named when he first saw them under his microscope; they later became known as protozoa and bacteria.

Bacteria:
Single-celled microorganisms that live in soil, water, plants, and animals and that play a key role in the decaying of organic matter and the cycling of nutrients. Some are agents of disease.

experiment
CENTRAL

Words to Know

Bacteriology:
The scientific study of bacteria, their characteristics, and their activities as related to medicine, industry, and agriculture.

Colony:
A mass of microorganisms that have been bred in a medium.

Control experiment:
A set-up that is identical to the experiment but is not affected by the variable that affects the experimental group.

Cultures:
Microorganisms growing in prepared nutrients.

Germ theory of disease:
The belief that disease is caused by germs.

Hypothesis:
An idea phrased in the form of a statement that can be tested by observation and/or experiment.

Lactobacilli:
A strain of bacteria.

Pasteur applied his theory to the wine industry and showed wine growers in his hometown that bad-tasting wine occurred when bacteria fell into wine as it was being bottled. Pasteur advised them how to heat bottled wine just enough to kill bacteria. This method, known as **pasteurization**, is still used in the wine and milk industries.

Between 1865 and 1870, Pasteur also discovered what was killing off France's silkworms. Under a microscope, he saw microorganisms infecting the sick silkworms as well as the leaves they were eating. After Pasteur recommended that the infected silkworms and leaves be destroyed, the unaffected ones thrived. These incidents supported Pasteur's **germ theory of disease**, that microorganisms cause diseases. He advanced the field of **bacteriology**, the study of different groups of bacteria.

These little guys do a lot

Tiny microorganisms are basically everywhere—in the air, in your body, in your cat's or dog's fur, and in the soil. Bacteria are the smallest single-celled organisms. To help us see them, today's microscopes can magnify subjects up to 2,000 times. That's ten times stronger than the microscope van Leeuwenhoek developed, which was quite an accomplishment for his time. We usually group all microorganisms together as disease-carrying germs, but many are important to life functions.

Microorganisms are categorized into five major groups: bacteria, such as salmonella; algae, such as blue-green algae; fungi, such as yeast; **protists**, such as amoebas; and viruses, such as chickenpox. Microorganisms are essential in the production of antibiotics, pickles, cheeses, and alcoholic beverages. Yeasts, which are in the fungi group, are used in bread and cheese making. The fungi group includes a mold

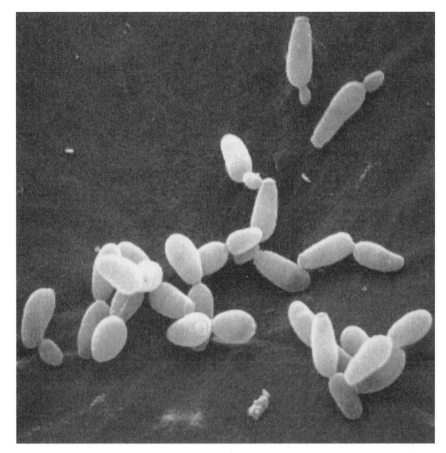

Microorganisms come in a wide range of shapes but are too tiny to see with the naked eye. (Photo Researchers Inc. Reproduced by permission.)

called **penicillin,** which is an antibiotic. Bacteria, protozoa, and fungi feed on dead, decaying organisms, such as the organic material placed into composters.

We cannot see microorganisms with the naked eye unless they multiply. Conducting some experiments will put us in touch with these amazing living creatures.

ⓦords to Know

Medium:
A material that contains the nutrients required for a particular micro-organism to grow.

Microbiology:
Branch of biology dealing with microscopic forms of life.

Microorganisms:
Living organisms so small that they can be seen only with the aid of a microscope.

Pasteurization:
The process of slow heating that kills many bacteria and other micro-organisms.

Penicillin:
A mold from the fungi group of microorganisms; used as an antibiotic.

Protists:
Members of the kingdom Protista, primarily single-celled organisms that are not plants or animals.

Experiment 1
Microorganisms: What is the best way to grow penicillin?

Purpose/Hypothesis
Penicillin is a microscopic mold that grows on fruit. It looks green and powdery and is shaped like a small paint brush when viewed under a

experiment
CENTRAL

Cheese curd is formed by adding bacteria to milk. (Photo Researchers Inc. Reproduced by permission.)

microscope. The word, *penicillin,* in fact, means "small brush" in Latin. Early writing was often done with a small, fine-pointed brush, and the English words pen and pencil are also derived from this Latin word.

In this experiment, you will determine the best growing conditions for the penicillin mold. You will place one set of fruit in a warm location and another set in a cool location. The difference in the amount of mold that grows will tell you whether temperature affects penicillin growth.

To begin the experiment, use what you know about mold growth to make an educated guess about the effect of temperature. This educated guess, or prediction, is your hypothesis. A hypothesis should explain these things:

- the topic of the experiment
- the **variable** you will change

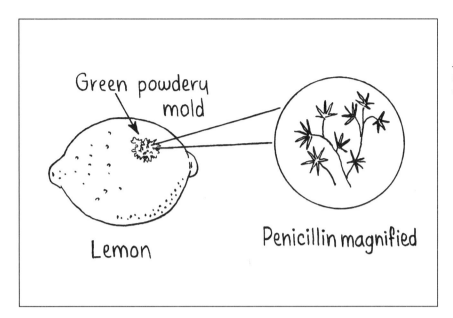

A moldy lemon (a small inset shows how mold looks under a microscope).

- the variable you will measure
- what you expect to happen

A hypothesis should be brief, specific, and measurable. It must be something you can test through observation. Your experiment will

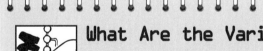

What Are the Variables?

Variables are anything that might affect the results of an experiment. Here are the main variables in this experiment:

- the type and age of the fruit
- the amount of bruising of the fruit
- temperature of the environment
- amount of light reaching the fruit
- humidity of the environment

In other words, the variables in this experiment are everything that might affect the growth of penicillin mold on the fruit. If you change more than one variable, you will not be able to tell which variable had the most effect on mold growth. Citrus fruits are the best source for this mold, so only citrus fruit will be used.

Words to Know

Protozoa:
Single-celled animal-like microscopic organisms that live by taking in food rather than making it by photosynthesis. They must live in the presence of water.

Variable:
Something that can affect the results of an experiment.

prove or disprove whether your hypothesis is correct. Here is one possible hypothesis for this experiment: "Penicillin mold will grow more rapidly and produce more visible mold under warm conditions."

In this case, the variable you will change is the temperature of the environment, and the variable you measure is the amount of visible mold that grows.

Level of Difficulty
Easy/moderate.

Materials Needed
- 2 cotton balls or small sponges
- 2 oranges, about equally ripe
- 2 lemons, about equally ripe
- 2 clear plastic bags (gallon size)
- bowl
- twist ties
- water
- use of a refrigerator
- microscopes and slides are optional

Approximate Budget
$2 for fruit and bags.

Timetable
20 minutes to set up, and 1 or 2 weeks to complete.

Step-by-Step Instructions
1. Bruise the fruit by rubbing it on the floor and dropping it. This helps the mold to invade the tough skin of the fruit.

2. Place the fruit in a bowl for 1 to 3 days. Leave the bowl out in the open where it will come into contact with mold in the air.

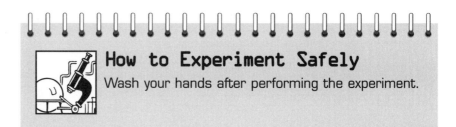

How to Experiment Safely
Wash your hands after performing the experiment.

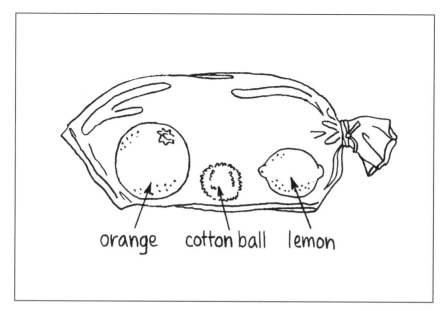

Steps 3 and 4: Place one orange, one lemon, and one moist cotton ball in clear plastic bag.

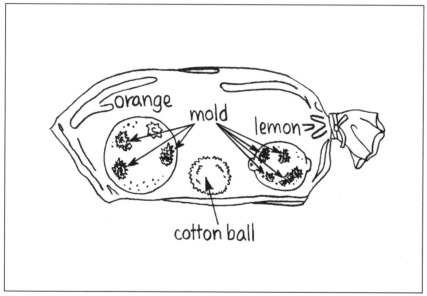

Step 8: After 2 weeks, open the bags and examine the fruit for mold.

3. In one bag place one orange, one lemon, and one moist cotton ball. (The moist cotton ball raises the humidity.)

4. Repeat step 3 for the other bag.

5. Tie each bag closed with a twist tie.

6. Place one bag in the refrigerator and the other in a warm place.

7. Every day, record any changes you observe.

Troubleshooter's Guide

Here is a problem that may arise during this experiment, a possible cause, and a way to remedy the problem.

Problem: Neither bag showed any mold growth after two weeks.

Possible cause: There was not enough humidity present in the bags. Remoisten the cotton balls and allow the experiment to run for an additional 2 weeks.

8. After 2 weeks, open the bags and examine the fruit.

9. If you have access to a microscope, smear a small sample of mold on a slide and view it.

Summary of Results
Compare the mold growth in each plastic bag. The bag in the warmer place should show considerably more growth because mold thrives in warm environments. Photograph your final results or draw a picture of what grew.

Change the Variables
You can conduct several similar experiments by changing the variables. For example, you can keep both bags of fruit at room temperature, but place one in normal room light and the other in a dark location to determine the effect of light on mold growth. You can also vary humidity by varying the number of soaked cotton balls or sponges. Remember, if you change more than one variable at a time, you will not be able to tell which variable had the most effect on mold growth.

Experiment 2
Growing Microorganisms in a Petri Dish

Purpose/Hypothesis
Microbiologists often breed microorganisms in large quantities called **colonies.** For this experiment you will prepare the **medium** needed to grow colonies of microorganisms.

experiment
CENTRAL

In this experiment you will change the source of the microorganisms. You will prepare the same medium for all samples. This medium is rich in nutrients needed by most microorganisms. You will then obtain microorganisms from different sources and observe their growth in the medium.

To begin the experiment, use what you know about the source of microorganisms to make an educated guess about whether different types will grow in the same medium. This educated guess, or prediction, is your **hypothesis.** A hypothesis should explain these things:

- the topic of the experiment
- the **variable** you will change
- the variable you will measure
- what you expect to happen

A hypothesis should be brief, specific, and measurable. It must be something you can test through observation. Your experiment will prove or disprove whether your hypothesis is correct. Here is one possible hypothesis for this experiment: "Different kinds of microorganisms can be obtained in many places, and all will thrive in a nutrient-

 ## What Are the Variables?

Variables are anything that might affect the results of an experiment. Here are the main variables in this experiment:

- the type of medium
- the temperature of the environment
- the humidity of the environment
- the amount of light reaching the petri dishes
- the sources of the microorganisms.

In other words, the variables in this experiment are everything that might affect the type and growth of microorganisms. If you change more than one variable, you will not be able to tell which variable had the most effect on the amount, color, and texture of the visible growth.

rich medium to produce visible growth that varies in amount, color, and texture."

In this case, the variable you will change is the source of the microorganisms, and the variable you measure is the amount, color, and texture of the visible growth that appears.

Level of Difficulty

Moderate. (This experiment requires special attention to cleanliness. Sterile conditions are ideal but almost impossible to obtain without training and special equipment.)

Materials Needed

- 6 petri dishes and lids (If petri dishes are not available, use small bowls and clear plastic wrap.)
- 1 package unflavored gelatin
- 1/4 cup (60 milliliters) sugar
- 1 tablespoon (15 milliliters) salt
- 1 tablespoon (15 milliliters) pork or beef, finely ground
- 1 1/2 quart (1.5 liter) pot with a cover
- 1 quart (1 liter) water
- tongs

Approximate Budget

$10 for petri dishes and food products.

Timetable

90 minutes to prepare, and 1 to 2 weeks for results.

Step-by-Step Instructions

1. In the pot, boil one quart of water.

2. When the water is boiling, use tongs to submerge the petri dishes into the water for 1 minute.

How to Experiment Safely

This experiment requires boiling hot water to cook gelatin and to sterilize the equipment. Ask an adult to help you when using the stove or when handling boiling water.

Petri dish tongs

Pot with
boiling water

*Steps 1 and 2: When the
water is boiling, use tongs
to submerge the petri dishes into the water for 1
minute.*

3. Remove the petri dishes from the water. Place on the counter or table. Place the lids on top to keep the inside clean. Allow them to cool.

4. Follow directions on the package to prepare gelatin.

5. Add sugar, salt, and finely ground meat.

6. Bring gelatin to quick boil and remove from the heat.

7. Cover and cool for 3 to 5 minutes.

8. Ask an adult to help you fill the six petri dishes halfway with the gelatin medium. Cover each dish immediately.

9. Cool 1 hour before moving.

10. To collect microorganisms from the environment, gently wipe a surface with a cotton swab. Here are some suggestions for samples: doorknob, arm, inside of mouth, floor, used cup, leftover food, dirt. Wipe five different surfaces—one for each of five petri dishes.

11. Gently rub each used swab on the gelatin in a dish. Do not touch more than one swab to a dish. You will not be able to see the microorganisms on the cotton swab. Trust that something is there.

12. Mark each dish with the date and the source of the sample. Cover each dish and seal it with tape.

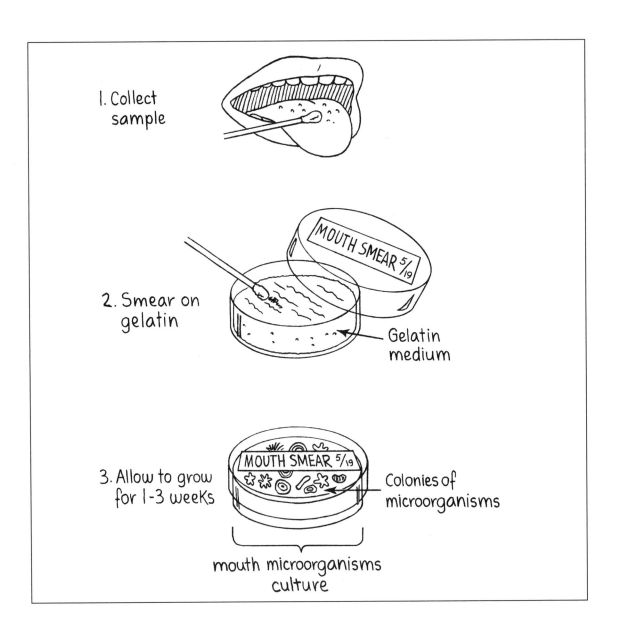

1. Collect sample

2. Smear on gelatin

MOUTH SMEAR 5/19

Gelatin medium

3. Allow to grow for 1-3 weeks

MOUTH SMEAR 5/19

Colonies of microorganisms

mouth microorganisms culture

Steps 10 to 12: Example of collecting microorganisms from the inside of the mouth. Be sure to collect samples from five different sources.

13. For a **control experiment,** leave one petri dish untouched. Label it "control" and seal it.

14. Keep the petri dishes together in a dark, warm area. Allow dishes to sit one to three weeks.

15. After the petri dishes show fuzzy gray mounds or slimy blobs, make a drawing of the microorganisms.

16. Do not open dishes or handle any microorganisms. Throw them away after the experiment.

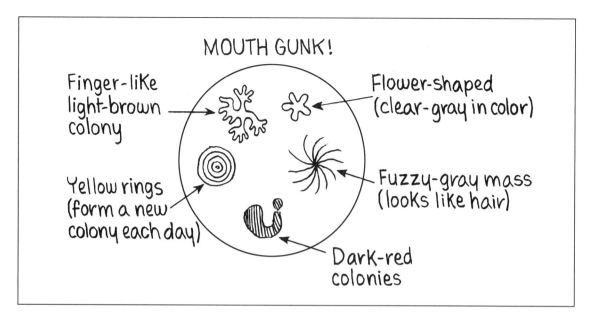

MOUTH GUNK!

Finger-like light-brown colony

Flower-shaped (clear-gray in color)

Yellow rings (form a new colony each day)

Fuzzy-gray mass (looks like hair)

Dark-red colonies

Step 15: Examples of microorganism colonies from mouth samples in petri dish after two weeks.

Summary of Results

Because of the complexity and variety of microorganisms, you cannot identify specific species. However, you should draw and describe your findings to share with others. Write a summary. Did colonies of microorganisms develop in all of your petri dishes? Were they different in color and texture? Did any growth appear in the control dish? Don't be surprised if it did. Even the air contains microorganisms. Were you able to support your hypothesis?

Change the Variables

After you have determined and recorded the amount, color, and texture of growth from various sources, repeat the experiment and change the

Troubleshooter's Guide

Here is a problem that may arise during this experiment, a possible cause, and a way to remedy the problem.

Problem: The microorganisms are not growing.

Possible cause: The conditions they need to grow are not in place. If after two weeks no growth is evident, try leaving the dishes in a warmer environment.

amount of light or the temperature or the humidity. Do some microorganisms grow more or less than before? Do they appear different from before? Remember, if you change more than one variable at a time, you will not be able to tell which variable had the most effect on growth.

 **Design Your Own Experiment**

How to Select a Topic Relating to this Concept

Microorganisms are everywhere. They are covering your body at this very moment, so you do not have to look far to find them. An experiment with microorganisms could include topics such as culturing or identifying their characteristics.

Check the For More Information section and talk with your science teacher or school or community media specialist to start gathering information on microorganism questions that interest you. As you consider possible experiments, be sure to discuss them with your science teacher or another knowledgeable adult before trying them. Some of the microorganisms or procedures might be dangerous.

Steps in the Scientific Method

To do an original experiment, you need to plan carefully and think things through. Otherwise, you might not be sure what question you are answering, what you are or should be measuring, or what your findings prove or disprove.

Here are the steps in designing an experiment:

- State the purpose of—and the underlying question behind—the experiment you propose to do.
- Recognize the variables involved, and select one that will help you answer the question at hand.
- State a testable hypothesis, an educated guess about the answer to your question.
- Decide how to change the variable you selected.
- Decide how to measure your results.

Recording Data and Summarizing the Results

The most important part of the experiment is the information gathered from it. Scientists working 400 years ago made discoveries in science that still help us today. In the fruit experiment, you cannot save the fruit to display or stop the decaying process with refrigeration. The results need to be recorded in drawings, photos, or notes. All these pieces of information you gathered then should be summarized into a conclusion or result.

Related Experiments

Microbes are simple organisms with simple needs, such as air (in some cases not even air), water, warm temperatures, and food. By putting microorganisms on a petri dish and adding a drop of different chemical cleaners, you can find out what substances keep them from growing. If it is safe, you may want to use that chemical when you wash. That's the idea behind antibacterial soaps.

For More Information

Dashefsky, H. Steven. *Microbiology: 49 Science Fair Projects.* Austin, TX: Tab Books, 1994. ❖ Outlines science projects that are well-suited for this topic.

Lang, S. *Invisible Bugs and Other Creepy Creatures That Live With You.* New York: Sterling Publishers, 1992. ❖ Describes different microorganisms, their functions, and purpose.

chapter 27

Mixtures and Solutions

Most of the substances we see around us are **mixtures,** combinations of different elements or compounds. The components of some mixtures—such as sandy water, which consists of grains of sand suspended in water—can easily be separated or will naturally settle. Others, such as salty water, form more permanent mixtures. How can we separate different kinds of mixtures into their component parts?

Mixtures that settle—separate out naturally— are called **suspensions.** Sandy water is a good example of a suspension. Stirring will mix the sand and the water, but over time, the denser sand will fall to the bottom of the container, and a clear layer of water will appear above it.

A mixture whose parts remain stable and remain mixed over time is called a **solution.** Solutions commonly consist of a solid **solute** that is *dissolved* in a liquid **solvent.** The molecules of the solute are evenly dispersed and very small. Salt water, lemon juice, and antifreeze are all solutions. These mixtures will remain mixed even when left standing for a long time.

A third type of mixture is a **colloid,** in which relatively large molecules of one substance remain mixed and stable due to **electric charge repulsions.** This repulsion occurs because colloidal particles contain an equal number of positive and negative ions (charged atoms), but the negative **ions** form a layer surrounding the particle. Thus, the particles are electrically neutral but still tend to repel one another to spread out evenly through the dispersing medium. Milk, gelatin, clay, and smoke are all colloids that combine solids, liquids, and gases in different ways.

Words to Know

Centrifuge:
A device that rapidly spins a solution so that the heavier components will separate from the lighter ones.

Coagulation:
The clumping together of particles in a mixture, often because the repelling force separating them is disrupted.

Colloid:
A mixture containing particles suspended in, but not dissolved in, a dispersing medium.

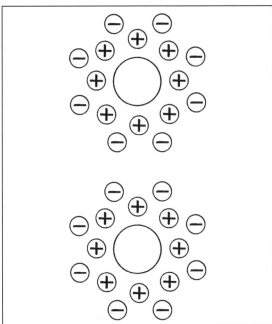

Words to Know

Control experiment: A set-up that is identical to the experiment but is not affected by the variable that affects the experimental group.

How mixtures can be separated

It is often necessary to separate mixtures into their component parts. Separating a suspension can be fairly simple. Suppose you lose a ring in a bucket of sandy water. Once the denser sand and the ring have settled to the bottom of the bucket, you can carefully pour off the clear water into another container. This process is known as **decanting.** Next, you can pour the soupy mixture of sand, water, and your ring into a strainer large enough to let the sand and water pass through. This process, known as **filtration,** will separate the ring from the other components of the suspension. Another means of separating mixtures is the **centrifuge,** which spins the mixture at high speeds until the more-dense particles are forced outward by centrifugal force and separate from the less-dense solvent.

Separating a solution is more difficult. For example, filtering salt out of seawater is possible only with extremely high pressure and very precise "molecular" filters. However, there are other ways to separate pure water from seawater. Raising the temperature of the solution until the water boils, capturing the steam and then cooling it until it condenses will yield pure liquid water and solid solute. This process is called **distillation.** Another process is called **evaporation,** which allows the vaporized water to escape, yielding only the solute.

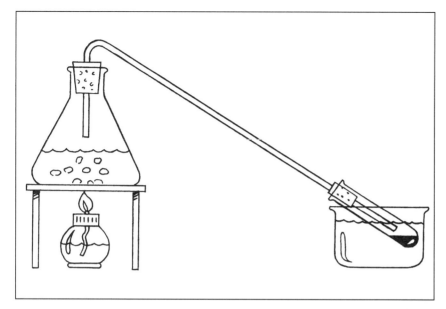

Words to Know

Decanting:
The process of separating a suspension by waiting for its heavier components to settle out and then pouring off the lighter ones.

Distillation:
The process of separating liquids from solids or from other liquids with different boiling points by a method of evaporation and condensation, so that each component in a mixture can be collected separately in its pure form.

Electric charge repulsion:
Repulsion of particles caused by a layer of negative ions surrounding each particle. The repulsion prevents coagulation and promotes the even dispersion of such particles through a mixtures.

Colloids can also be separated into their component parts. When a colloid is heated, the repelling force between the colloidal particles is no longer great enough to keep the heated particles from bouncing into each other and bonding together. They gradually form clumps and settled out of the mixture. Causing colloidal particles to gather is called **coagulation.** It can be seen clearly in milk, which forms clumps of fat, called curds, when heated.

Knowing how to separate mixtures into their component parts is crucial in both science and everyday life. Removing spaghetti from a pot of boiling water is not easy without filtration. Coagulation allows ionic or electrostatic cleaners to remove dust and soot from the air we breathe. A centrifuge is used to separate blood into its vital parts without damaging them. In the first experiment, you will identify various mixtures as suspension or solutions by applying different separation techniques.

Although liquid colloids can often behave just like suspensions, there is a simple method for distinguishing between them. A light beam passing through a solution will not encounter any particles large enough to deflect it, and thus will not be visible. Colloidal particles are not dissolved and can be quite large compared to the particles in a suspension. A light beam passing through a colloid will be visible as it is dispersed by these particles. This phenomenon is called the **Tyndall effect.** In the second project, you will use the Tyndall effect to distinguish a colloidal mixture from a solution.

Experiment 1

Suspensions and Solutions: Can filtration and evaporation determine whether mixtures are suspensions or solutions?

Purpose/Hypothesis

In this experiment, you will attempt to separate the component parts of several mixtures using two different methods. The result of each method will determine the nature of the mixture. One mixture will consist of sand in distilled water, and the other will be lemon juice in distilled water. Before you begin, make an educated guess about the outcome of this experiment based on your knowledge of mixtures. This educated guess, or prediction, is your **hypothesis.** A hypothesis should explain these things:

- the topic of the experiment
- the variable you will change
- the variable you will measure
- what you expect to happen

A hypothesis should be brief, specific, and measurable. It must be something you can test through observation. Your experiment will

What Are the Variables?

Variables are anything that might affect the results of an experiment. Here are the main variables in this experiment:

- the type of mixtures tested
- the purity of the mixed components
- size of the openings in the filter
- the temperature of the mixture

In other words, the variables in this experiment are everything that might affect the ability of a component to be separated from a mixture. If you change more than one variable, you will not be able to tell which variable had the most effect on the separation.

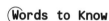

Words to Know

tion and exists in the least amount in a solution, for example sugar in sugar water.

Solution:
A mixture of two or more substances that appears to be uniform throughout.

Solvent:
The major component of a solution or the liquid in which some other component is dissolved, for example water in sugar water.

Suspension:
A temporary mixture of a solid in a gas or liquid from which the solid will eventually settle out.

Tyndall effect:
The effect achieved when colloidal particles reflect a beam of light, making it visible when shined through such a mixture.

Variable:
Something that can affect the results of an experiment.

prove or disprove whether your hypothesis is correct. Here is one possible hypothesis for this experiment: "A solid mixed into a liquid may be separated by filtration if the mixture is a suspension, such as sand in water, or by evaporation if the mixture is a solution, such as lemon juice in water."

In this case, the **variable** you will change is the component mixed with water, and the variable you will measure is ability of a specific method to separate the components. You expect that filtration will separate the sand, thus showing it is a suspension, and evaporation will separate the lemon juice, thus showing it is a solution.

You will also set up a **control experiment** of pure water, with no substances mixed into it, to which you will apply the same methods of separation for comparison.

Level of Difficulty

Moderate, because of the time involved and the care required when using a heat source.

Materials Needed

- 2 small saucepans, about 5 inches (12.5 centimeters) in diameter
- heat source (stove or a Bunsen burner)
- 4 clear 1-quart (1-liter) wide-mouth bottles

- 6 lemons
- 3 cups distilled water
- 1 cup (225 grams) of sand
- knife
- tablespoon
- funnel
- 3 conical paper coffee filters
- large wooden cutting board

Approximate Budget

Less than $5, assuming a Bunsen burner or a stove is available.

Timetable

The first stage of this experiment requires at least 1 hour for set-up, filtration, and partial evaporation by boiling. The second stage, evaporation without boiling, may take several hours or days, depending upon how much liquid remains in the saucepans.

Step-by-Step Instructions

1. Carefully cut the lemons in half and squeeze their juice into a bottle. Do not remove any solid particles or seeds from the juice. Add 1 cup of distilled water and set the bottle aside.

2. Pour 1 cup of distilled water into another bottle and stir in 3 tablespoons of sand.

3. In a third bottle, place 1 cup of distilled water. This will be your control experiment.

4. Filter the lemon juice. Place a coffee filter inside the funnel, hold the funnel over a bottle, and slowly pour the lemon juice into the

How to Experiment Safely

This experiment involves heat and boiling liquid. These steps should be performed with adult supervision and with proper protection, including potholders. Do not substitute other mixtures for those in this experiment without consulting your teacher. Many substances can ignite or give off toxic fumes when heated.

Appearance After			
Mixture		Stirring	Filtering	Evaporation
	lemon/ water	cloudy w/ visible particles		
	sand/ water	cloudy		
	control (water)	clear		

Step 5: Sample data chart for Experiment 1.

funnel. The liquid that passes through the filter should appear uniform but will not be clear. Discard the used filter and clean the funnel and bottle, rinsing them with distilled water.

5. Prepare a chart on which you will record your observations. Your chart should look something like the illustration.

6. Stir each of the three samples, making sure to clean the spoon or stirrer after each one. Note the appearance of each sample on your chart.

7. Allow the mixtures to settle for several minutes. In the next column on your chart, note any change in appearance.

8. Line the funnel with another coffee filter and place it over the opening of the fourth bottle. Pour the mixture of water and sand into the funnel. Allow the liquid to filter into the bottle. Note any change in appearance on your chart. (See page 410.)

9. Pour the lemon-juice mixture into a saucepan and place the saucepan on the heat source. Do not leave this sample unattended.

Step 8: Pour the mixture slowly and carefully into the funnel, as it may not drain quickly through the coffee filter.

Observe the sample as it evaporates. Do not allow the liquid to evaporate completely!

10. When only a few tablespoons of the liquid remain, remove the saucepan from the heat and place it carefully on the wooden cutting board. (Remember to turn off the heat source when not using it and to be cautious around the saucepan, which will cool slowly.)

11. Repeat step 9 with your control liquid (the distilled water sample) in the second saucepan.

12. Place both saucepans in a safe place. Do not cover them. The liquids must continue to evaporate for you to see any dissolved solids. This final evaporation may take hours or even days, depending on how much liquid is left.

13. Check the samples periodically. Once the liquid in the lemon juice has completely evaporated, note on your chart whether any visible solids have been left behind on the surface of the saucepan. Also monitor your control experiment. It should leave no significant solid residue in the pan. If it does, then your results cannot prove your hypothesis.

Summary of Results

Examine your results and determine whether your hypothesis is true. If a solid in a mixture is removed by your filtration method, then it was in suspension, and not in solution. If a solid is not removed by filtration but is removed by evaporation, then the solid was in solution. Compare your results for the control, the sand mixture, and the lemon mixture. Write a summary of your findings.

Troubleshooter's Guide

Here is a problem that may arise during this experiment, a possible cause, and a way to remedy the problem.

Problem: The sand and water sample will not pass through the filter.

Possible cause: The sand is preventing the water from passing through the funnel. Set the apparatus aside and allow time for the water to filter slowly through the sand and the filter. This may take awhile.

Change the Variables

You can conduct similar experiments by changing the variables. For example, try different mixtures. Do not use any solvent other than water. Compare your results for mixtures using salt, flour, gelatin, bouillon cubes, or effervescent antacid tablets. You can also experiment with the effect of temperature. Some solids, such as sugar, will dissolve more easily when the water is hot than when it is cool.

Project 2
Colloids: Can colloids be distinguished from suspension using the Tyndall effect?

Purpose

In this project, you will demonstrate how the Tyndall effect can be used to show that a mixture that looks like a solution is actually a colloid.

Level of Difficulty

Moderate.

Materials Needed

- flashlight
- black construction paper
- tape
- 0.5 pint (0.25 liter) heavy cream

- lemon juice
- 12-ounce (0.33-liter) soda
- 1 quart (1 liter) distilled water
- 0.5 teaspoon measuring spoon
- 5 clear glass jars

Approximate Budget

$10 to $15. (Most materials may be found in the average household.)

Timetable

Less than 1 hour.

Step-by-Step Instructions

1. Pour 1 cup of distilled water into each jar. Add 0.5 teaspoon of heavy cream to the first jar and stir vigorously. Clean the spoon with distilled water.

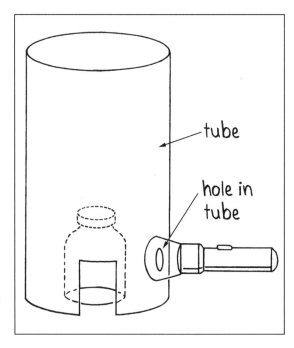

Step 7: Construct a shield to block other illumination from reaching the jar.

2. Add 0.5 teaspoon of lemon juice, salt, and soda to the second, third, and fourth jars respectively. Remember to stir each one and to wash the spoon to avoid mixing the samples. The fifth jar, the control, should contain only distilled water.

3. Curl a sheet of construction paper into a cone, leaving a 1-inch (2.5-centimeter) diameter opening. Tape

	water/cream	water/lemon	water/salt	water/soda	control
appearance in normal light:					
appearance in Tyndall Effect test:					
colloid? y/n:					

Step 8: Data chart for Experiment 2.

the cone to the flashlight so it narrows the beam through the small opening.

4. Darken the room or an area of the room. (Total darkness is not necessary or safe.) Set the control jar of distilled water on a flat, clear surface. Shine the light through the jar from one side and observe that the light does not illuminate the water itself.

5. Try shining the light through the milk mixture. If the path of the beam is visible in the liquid, the mixture is a colloid. If the beam is not visible, the mixture is a solution.

6. Repeat step 5 with the other mixtures.

Troubleshooter's Guide

This project is fairly simple, so not many problems should arise. However, when doing experiments involving mixtures, be aware that a number of unseen variables—such as temperature and impurity of substances—can affect your results. When mixing substances for a demonstration or experiment, you must keep the mixing containers and utensils clean. Even tiny impurities in a mixture can drastically alter your results. Any experiment you perform must be carefully designed to avoid letting unknown variations change the outcome and lead you to an incorrect conclusion.

Here is a problem that may arise during this project, some possible causes, and ways to remedy the problem.

Problem: All of the mixtures appear to scatter the light beam.

Possible causes:

1. Too much light is reaching the back, top, or sides of the jar. Try isolating the jars by constructing the light shield described in step 7.

2. Your samples have become corrupted. Prepare new samples, making sure to clean the spoon between each mixture.

7. If you find it difficult to determine when the light beam is being scattered, construct a shield to block other illumination from reaching the jar. Curl a sheet of construction paper into a tube. Cut an opening at the front through which you can observe, and a hole at the side through which you can shine the light beam. Place the tube over the jar and repeat steps 4 and 5 to see the difference between a light beam when it is scattered and when it is not scattered.

8. Create a chart to show the results of your demonstration, noting which mixtures are colloids and which are solutions.

Summary of Results

Remember that those who view your results may not have seen the project demonstrations performed, so you must present the information you have gathered in as clear a way as possble. Illustrations can show viewers the steps involved in determining whether a mixture is a solution or a colloid.

 # Design Your Own Experiment

How to Select a Topic Related to this Concept

The nature of mixtures can provide topics for fascinating experiments and projects. Try measuring the changes that occur in the temperature at which water boils and when salt is added to it. You might test other methods of purification. Can you construct a simple centrifuge to separate suspensions? Can you purify salt water by freezing as well as by boiling? Finding the answers to these questions can become the basis for simple yet informative projects.

Check the For More Information section and talk with your science teacher or school or community media specialist to start gathering information on mixture questions that interest you. Remember to check with a knowledgeable person before experimenting with unfamiliar materials.

Steps in the Scientific Method

To do an original experiment, you need to plan carefully and think things through. Otherwise, you might not be sure what question you are answering, what you are or should be measuring, or what your findings prove or disprove.

Here are the steps in designing an experiment:

- State the purpose of—and the underlying question behind—the experiment you propose to do.
- Recognize the variables involved, and select one that will help you answer the question at hand.
- State your hypothesis, an educated guess about the answer to your question.
- Recognize the variables involved and select one that will help you answer the question at hand.
- Decide how to change the variable you have selected.
- Decide how to measure your results.

Recording Data and Summarizing the Results

In the experiments included here and in any experiments you develop, you can try to display your data in more accurate and interesting ways. For example, in the colloid project, you could redesign the demonstration to show the light-beam test simultaneously for all of the jars.

Remember that those who view your results may not have seen the experiment performed, so you must present the information you have gathered in as clear a way as possible. Including photographs or illustrations of the steps in the experiment is a good way to show a viewer how you got from your hypothesis to your conclusion.

Related Projects

The isolation of substances in mixtures is an important and challenging part of chemistry. Other methods besides those described here can provide ideas for projects and experiments. For example, mixtures of two solids can be separated by using magnetism. Mixtures of two liquids that have different boiling points can be separated using distillation. Investigate these methods in the books listed in For More Information, and try incorporating them into other projects.

For More Information

Gillett, Kate, ed. *The Knowledge Factory*. Brookfield, CT: Copper Beech Books, 1996. ❖ Provides some fun and enlightening observations on questions relevant to this topic, along with good ideas for projects and demonstrations.

Ray, C. Claibourne. *The New York Times Book of Science Questions and Answers*. New York: Doubleday, 1997. ❖ Addresses both everyday observations and advanced scientific concepts on a wide variety of subjects.

experiment
CENTRAL

Van Cleave, Janice. *Chemistry For Every Kid.* New York: John Wiley and Sons, Inc., 1989. ❖ Contains simple and informative demonstrations of colloid coagulation and the principle of the centrifuge.

Wolke, Robert L. *What Einstein Didn't Know: Scientific Answers to Everyday Questions.* Secaucus, NJ: Birch Lane Press, 1997. ❖ Contains a number of entries relevant to mixtures and solutions.

chapter 28

Nutrition

The foods you eat affect whether you pay attention in class, how much energy you have for sports, and even whether you feel happy or sad. In fact, your meals and snacks affect how every cell in your body works. How do we know? **Nutrition** is the science of how the body uses nutrients to grow and function effectively. **Nutrients** are nourishing substances that the body needs. For example, the heart needs certain nutrients to help it pump blood. Our kidneys need nutrients to help rid our bodies of harmful wastes. Not surprisingly, deficiencies in certain nutrients can cause disease.

Real men eat fruit

Hardly anyone gets **scurvy** anymore, but this disease was common a few centuries ago, especially among the first explorers and the crews on their ships. No one knew what caused scurvy. People with it felt weak. Their gums, noses, and mouths bled, and their muscles ached. When the ship of French explorer Jacques Cartier became icebound on the St. Lawrence River in Montreal in 1535, twenty-five men became ill and died. Cartier was visited by local Native Americans. He mentioned his feelings of weakness and the bleeding symptoms of his men. The Native Americans went into the woods, brought back pine needles and bark from a tree, and told Cartier to boil them in water. Cartier and his men drank the tea and recovered.

We now know the pine needles contained vitamin C, a substance also present in fruits and vegetables. Fruits and vegetables were rarely eaten on ships at that time. Storing them was a problem, and they were expensive to buy.

Words to Know

Amine:
An organic compound derived from ammonia.

Amino acid:
One of a group of organic compounds that make up proteins.

Antibody:
A protein produced by certain cells of the body as an immune (disease-fighting) response to a specific foreign antigen.

Antigen:
A substance that causes the production of an antibody when injected directly into the body.

In 1747, James Lind, a Scottish doctor, knew that many British sailors were dying from scurvy, but he had read a report that fruits and vegetables helped prevent the disease. The sailors recovered quickly when Lind added citrus fruit juices to their diet, so Lind suggested this remedy to the British navy. Still, it took several decades before this remedy was taken seriously. Eventually, scurvy was all but eliminated.

Eat right to stay healthy

It was not until the early 1900s that scientists began to understand how nutrient deficiencies affect the body. The body cannot make all the substances it needs, but those missing substances are found in food. Before we realized this, however, these substances were often removed from food.

In the early 1900s, many foods were being processed. When rice processors removed the bran layers from whole rice to make white rice, they did not realize they were also removing a substance that was necessary for the body to function well. In regions where rice was the main food, a deficiency in this substance was causing a disease called **beriberi**. In 1911, Polish researcher Casimir Funk isolated this substance and discovered a type of chemical compound called an **amine**. He linked it with the Latin word *vita*, meaning "life," and the new term **vitamin** was created. The vitamin in bran was named **thiamine**, a B vitamin that helps the body obtain energy from carbohydrates.

As they learned more, scientists concluded that eating a variety of foods that are not processed, such as meats, fish, and fresh fruits and vegetables, helps our bodies stay healthy. And taking extra vitamins does not hurt either.

Dr. James Lind suggested eating citrus fruits to prevent scurvy. (Bettmann Archive. Reproduced by permission.)

Compared to the unhealthy chick, the healthy chick, right, received a sufficient amount of B and C vitamins in its diet. (Grant Heilman. Reproduced by permission.)

The necessary nutrients

Besides vitamins, what are the other main substances your body needs to work well? One is **carbohydrates,** which give your body energy. They are present in starches, including potatoes, rice, bread, peas, and beans. They are also in milk and fruit, as well as in fiber from grains and vegetables. Your body uses carbohydrates to manufacture the zip you need to win a race or hit a home run.

Fats are necessary, too. Fats that come from olive oil, yogurt, nuts, and cheese help you grow and make your skin smooth. Fats also cushion body organs, keep your body warm, and help you absorb vitamins. Extra fats are stored under the skin and become another source of energy when needed.

Minerals, another kind of essential nutrient, help build bones and soft tissues. They act as regulators, keeping your blood pressure stable and your heart rate steady. They also keep your bones and teeth tough and help you digest your food. The six main minerals your body requires are calcium, magnesium, phosphorus, potassium, sodium, and sulfur. These minerals can be found in dairy products, fruit, vegetables, and meats. Other minerals, just as important but needed in smaller quantities, are known as **trace elements.** Some of the more important ones are iron, fluorine, iodine, and zinc.

Peas and beans are good sources of carbohydrates. (Grant Heilman. Reproduced by permission.)

Words to Know

Protein:
A complex chemical compound that consists of many amino acids attached to each other that are essential to the structure and functioning of all living cells.

Scurvy:
A disease caused by a deficiency of vitamin C, which causes a weakening of connective tissue in bone and muscle.

Thiamine:
A vitamin of the B complex that is essential to normal metabolism and nerve function.

Trace element:
A chemical element present in minute quantities.

Translucent:
Permits the passage of light.

Vitamin:
A complex organic compound found naturally in plants and animals that the body needs in small amounts for normal growth and activity.

Your body needs help making cells as you grow and replacing cells that become worn out. That's where proteins come in. Besides helping to build new cells, proteins trigger and speed up reactions within your body. Proteins also help form **antibodies** that ward off infections. Soybeans, beef, fish, beans, eggs, peas, and whole wheat are sources of protein.

You might not think that water would be an important nutrient, but it is. Nutrients can be carried to where they are needed only in watery solutions.

Good nutrition is essential for good health. Eating a variety of fresh, nonprocessed foods helps prevent diseases and sickness and gives you energy to work, think, and play. The projects that follow will help you analyze what you are actually eating on a day-to-day basis.

Project 1
Energizing Foods: Which foods contain carbohydrates and fats?

Purpose

This project will help you analyze a typical meal to discover which foods provide the energy we need for our day-to-day activities. You will test for fats and for starches. Fats supply energy and are stored in the body for times when energy levels are low, such as when you exercise or miss a meal. The starches in carbohydrates also provide energy.

Level of Difficulty

Easy.

Materials Needed

- iodine with dropper
- brown paper bags cut into 10 or more 4-inch (10-centimeter) squares
- clear glass dinner plate
- a typical meal (For example, a lunch consisting of a turkey and Swiss cheese sandwich with tomato, lettuce, and mayonnaise; milk; potato chips. Or a dinner of hamburger, pasta salad, corn bread, milk, and cake with icing)

Approximate Budget

$2 for iodine; other supplies from meals.

Timetable

1 hour; this project can be repeated after each meal to determine eating trends.

Step-by-Step Instructions

1. Create two 1 teaspoon-sized samples of each food, such as two samples of turkey, two of Swiss cheese, two of bread, and so on.

2. To test the foods for fat, rub a food sample on a square of brown paper. Remove the food sample, and allow the paper to dry.

How to Work Safely

Be careful not to get the iodine in your eyes. Ask an adult to help you use the iodine.

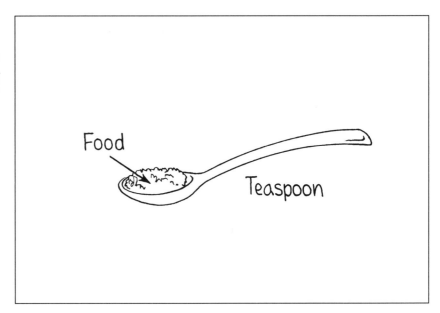

Step 1: Create two 1 teaspoon-sized samples of each food.

Food

Teaspoon

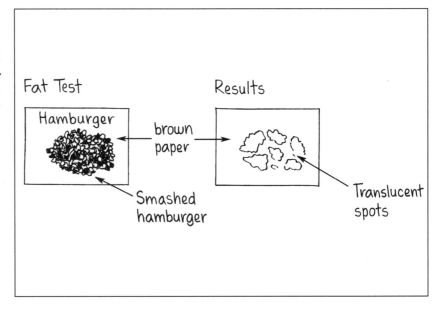

Steps 2 and 3: To test the foods for fat, rub a food sample on a square of brown paper. Remove the food sample, and allow the paper to dry.

Fat Test

Results

Hamburger

brown paper

Smashed hamburger

Translucent spots

3. Hold the paper up to the light and notice if it is translucent (if you can see light through it). Describe your observations on a data chart. Make a plus sign under a Fats heading for those foods that leave a translucent stain.

4. To test for starch, place a food sample on the glass dinner plate. Drip 4 to 5 drops of iodine onto the food. Allow 15 minutes for the iodine to penetrate.

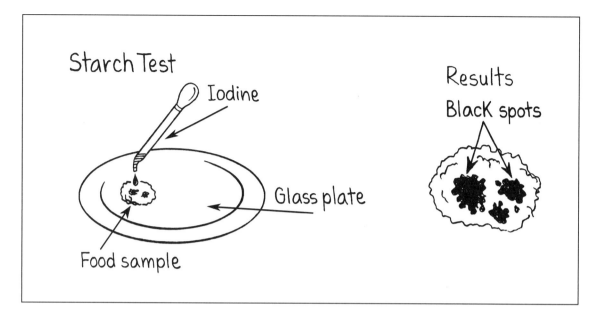

5. On your data chart, make a plus sign under a Starch heading for foods that turn black from the iodine.

6. Repeat Steps 2 through 5 for each kind of food. Place each sample in a different spot on the paper and on the plate.

Steps 4 and 5: Test food samples for starch by dripping 4 to 5 drops of iodine onto the food.

Summary of Results

Analyze your results. Figure out how many foods in your meal contain starch and/or fat. Consider what this says about the healthfulness of the meal and of your diet in general.

 Troubleshooter's Guide

Here is a problem that may arise during this project, a possible cause, and a way to remedy the problem.

Problem: Apples or pears do not stain black with iodine.

Possible cause: These fruits contain cellulose, which is plant starch. Iodine turns black with more soluble, digestible starches, such as wheat, rice, and beans.

Project 2
Nutrition: Which foods contain proteins and salts?

Purpose
This project will help you identify proteins and salts, nutrients needed for cell repair and daily maintenance. Proteins, present in every cell, are known as body builders. They help you grow and replace cells. Salts are minerals that your body uses to maintain water balance.

Level of Difficulty
Moderate. This experiment requires the purchase of two chemicals and the supervision of an adult.

Materials Needed
- silver nitrate (a salt-indicator solution, which can be purchased from science supply catalogs)
- Biuret solution (a protein-indicator solution, also available from science supply catalogs)
- glass test tubes or glass cups
- test tube rack
- food from one meal
- water
- goggles
- rubber gloves

Approximate Budget
$20 for the silver nitrate and Biuret solutions, depending on the quantity. The silver nitrate can be purchased as a crystal and dissolved in water.

 ## How to Work Safely
Ask an adult to help you with this project. Wear goggles or other eye protection and protective gloves when handling silver nitrate. Be careful with the silver nitrate, as it stains the skin.

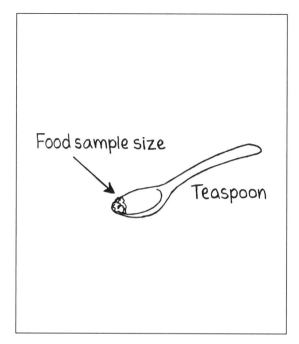

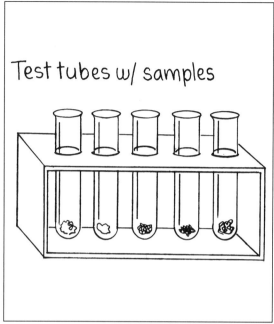

Timetable

1 hour.

Step-by-Step Instructions

1. Create 1/4-teaspoon-size samples of each type of food from your meal.

2. Set test tubes in rack.

3. For the protein test, put a food sample into a test tube and add 10 drops of Biuret solution.

4. Wait 10 minutes. If the blue Biuret solution turns lavender, the sample contains protein. Record the result on a data chart.

5. For the salt test, put a food sample into a test tube and fill tube halfway with water. Shake gently. Add 10-20 drops of silver nitrate solution.

6. Watch to see if the clear silver nitrate forms a milky white precipitation in the water. If so, salt is present. Record your results.

7. Repeat Steps 3 through 6 for each food sample, recording all your results on the data sheet.

LEFT: Step 1: Create 1/4-teaspoon-size samples of each type of food from your meal.

RIGHT: Step 3: Place a food sample into each test tube.

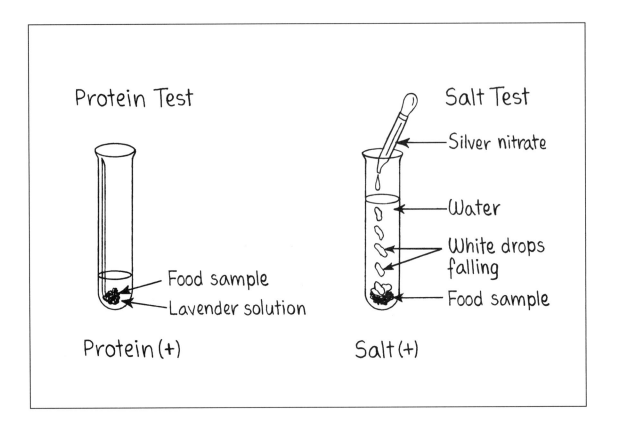

Protein Test

Salt Test

Silver nitrate

Water

White drops
falling

Food sample

Food sample
Lavender solution

Protein (+)

Salt (+)

*Steps 3 to 6: Testing food
samples for either protein
or salt content.*

Summary of Results

After testing a typical meal, analyze your results. How many samples contained protein or salt? Do you see any pattern? Write a paragraph summarizing your findings.

Troubleshooter's Guide

Here is a problem that may arise during this experiment, a possible cause, and a way to remedy the problem.

Problem: None of my foods tested positive for salt.

Possible cause: Insignificant amounts of salt may be present. Make a test tube sample of salt and water. Add silver nitrate to see if the solution turns white. If not, the silver nitrate may be contaminated.

experiment
CENTRAL

Design Your Own Experiment

How to Select a Topic Relating to this Concept

Diet is such a vital part of a healthy lifestyle that studying your eating habits is important. You might decide to research the major nutrients and learn more about how they can help improve your health.

Check the For More Information section and talk with your science teacher or school or community media specialist to gather information on nutrition questions that interest you. As you consider possible experiments, be sure to discuss them with a knowledgeable adult before trying them.

Steps in the Scientific Method

To do an original experiment, you need to plan carefully and think things through. Otherwise, you might not be sure what question you are answering, what your are or should be measuring, or what your findings prove or disprove.

Here are the steps in designing an experiment:

- State the purpose of—and the underlying question behind—the experiment you propose to do.
- Recognize the variables involved, and select one that will help you answer the question at hand.
- State a testable hypothesis, an educated guess about the answer to your question.
- Decide how to change the variable you selected.
- Decide how to measure your results.

Recording Data and Summarizing the Results

It's always important to write down data and ideas you gather during an experiment. Keep a journal or record book for this purpose. If you keep notes and draw conclusions from your experiments and projects, other scientists could use your findings in their own research.

Related Projects

Nutrition-related projects or experiments can go in many different directions. For example, you might identify the types and quantity of nutrients you eat daily. You might decide to start regulating your intake of the less-healthful foods. As a start, all you need to do is read the nutritional facts found on all food packages.

For More Information

Eating for Health. Vol. 3. Chicago: World Book Inc., 1993. ❖ Part of the *Growing Up* series, this volume provides thorough, interesting information about carbohydrates, vitamins, and minerals as well as metabolism, eating disorders, and processing.

Levchuck, Caroline, and Michele Drohan. *Healthy Living.* Detroit: U•X•L, 2000. ❖ Contains chapters on nutrition, eating disorders, and other health issues.

experiment
CENTRAL

chapter 29

Optics and Optical Illusions

Do you ever wonder how your eyes allow you to see? The science of light waves and how we see them is called **optics.** To understand optics, you must first understand a little about light itself.

What is light made of?

Visible light is a series of **electromagnetic waves.** These waves make up a small part of the **electromagnetic spectrum,** which includes many kinds of energy waves. You may be familiar with some of these, such as radio waves, microwaves, and X rays. Visible light is made of waves that are about 0.000014 to 0.000027 inches (360 to 700 nanometers) long. A **nanometer** is one-billionth of a meter. In this range are all the colors we can see; each color has a slightly different wavelength.

Light does all kinds of interesting things. It can bounce off surfaces, particularly smooth surfaces. This is called **reflection.** It can also bend as it moves from one kind of material to another, such as from air to water. (That's why a pencil sticking out of a glass of water looks bent.) This is called **refraction.**

How do our eyes perceive light?

The eye has a **lens** that focuses light onto a light-sensitive surface at the back of the eyeball, called the **retina.** The retina then sends nerve impulses to the brain, which the brain interprets as images.

The lens in your eye is made of membranes and fluid, while the artificial lenses used in telescopes and cameras are glass or plastic. A lens must be made of a transparent material so that it can transmit a beam of light, forming an image.

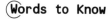

Words to Know

Concave:
Hollowed or rounded inward, like the inside of a bowl.

Convex:
Curved or rounded outward, like the outside of a ball.

Electromagnetic spectrum:
The complete array of electromagnetic radiation, including radio waves (at the longest-wavelength end), microwaves, infrared radiation, visible light, ultraviolet radiation, X rays, and gamma rays (at the shortest-wavelength end).

experiment
CENTRAL

A prism separates the colors in sunlight so we can see them. (Photo Researchers Inc. Reproduced by permission.)

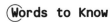
What questions do you have about light and how we see it? You will have an opportunity to explore optics in the experiments that follow.

Experiment 1
Optics: What is the focal length of a lens?

Purpose/Hypothesis
In this experiment, you will identify the **focal point** of different lenses and measure their **focal lengths**. When light rays pass through a lens, they converge at a single point, the focal point of the lens. The distance from the middle of the lens to the focal point is called the focal length. Every lens has its own focal length.

The focal length of a lens indicates where the image will be focused and how powerful the lens is. In general, a lens has two rounded sur-

faces and its edges are fairly thin compared to its diameter. Focal length depends on the curvature of these surfaces. A **convex** lens has surfaces that curve outward, like a ball, while a **concave** lens has surfaces that curve inward, like the inside of a bowl.

The lens in a camera focuses light from a subject you are photographing onto the camera film. (Photo Researchers Inc. Reproduced by permission.)

Before you begin, make an educated guess about the outcome of this experiment based on your knowledge of optics. This educated guess, or prediction, is your **hypothesis**. A hypothesis should explain these things:

- the topic of the experiment
- the variable you will change
- the variable you will measure
- what you expect to happen

A hypothesis should be brief, specific, and measurable. It must be something you can test through observation. Your experiment will prove or disprove your hypothesis. Here is one possible hypothesis for this experiment: "The more convex the lens, the shorter the focal length."

experiment
CENTRAL

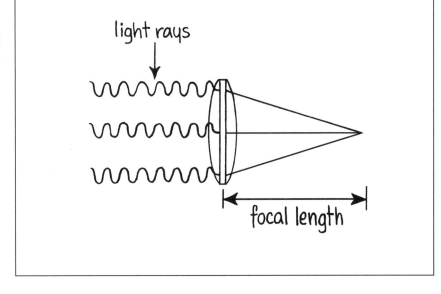

The focal length of a lens indicates where the image will be focused and how powerful the lens is.

In this case, the **variable** you will change will be the kind of lens, and the variable you will measure will be the focal length. You expect that lenses which are more convex will produce shorter focal lengths.

Level of Difficulty

Moderate, because of the materials needed.

What Are the Variables?

Variables are anything that might affect the results of an experiment. Here are the main variables in this experiment:

- the kind of lens being used

- the focal length of the lens

- the angle at which you hold the lens relative to the light source

- the distance from the object to lens

In other words, the variables in this experiment are everything that might affect the point at which the light focuses. If you change more than one variable, you will not be able to tell which variable had the most effect on the focal length.

Materials Needed

- 3 or 4 different lenses, labeled for convexity and concavity (You might borrow them from school or buy them at a science museum shop.)
- ruler or tape measure
- large, white piece of paper or tagboard
- small lamp

Approximate Budget

$20 to purchase lenses.

Timetable

2 hours.

Step-by-Step Instructions

1. Choose a room where you can dim the lights and set up the experiment. Place your lamp at least 3 feet (1 meter) away from your first lens.

2. In the dim light, hold the white card on the other side of the lens and look for the image of your object (the lamp). If you cannot see it, move the card closer to or farther from the lens until you can find it. Keep adjusting the distance of the card until your image is focused.

3. Set up a data chart, and describe what you see. How does the image look in comparison to the actual object? Write down any differences you observe.

4. Measure and record the distance between the lens and the card on which the focused image appears. Be sure to note which lens you were using.

5. Repeat the above steps with your other lenses. Record your findings on your chart.

How to Experiment Safely

Do not drop the lenses, and try not to touch the lens surfaces with your fingers. Hands naturally have a lot of oils on them, which will affect how the lenses work.

Troubleshooter's Guide

Experiments do not always work out as planned. Even so, figuring out what went wrong can definitely be a learning experience. Here are some problems that may arise during this experiment, some possible causes, and ways to remedy the problems.

Problem: You cannot see an image at all.

Possible cause: Your room is not dark enough or your object is not bright enough. Try darkening the room more or choosing a brighter light source.

Problem: The focal length measurements are all alike.

Possible causes:

1. Your lenses are too similar. Check the lens labels and make sure you have lenses with different characteristics. Someone at the store where you purchased them should be able to help.

2. You are not looking closely enough at the image to see where it is in focus. Sometimes the focus can be subtle. Look more closely at your cards.

Summary of Results

Study the results on your chart. Which kind of lenses produced short focal lengths? Which produced longer ones? Was your hypothesis correct? Summarize what you have found.

Change the Variables

You can vary this experiment in several ways. For example, try varying where you place the object on the other side of the lens. Measure and record what you find. You can also try placing two or more lenses next to each other and observe the effect on the image. Do the lenses add their effects together or do they cancel each other out? Does the image change size or direction? Record what you find.

Experiment 2
Optical Illusions: Can the eye be fooled?

Purpose/Hypothesis

After the lenses in your eyes focus light, your brain must make sense of the images formed. This is not always easy. Optical illusions occur when the brain is tricked into thinking things are not as they are. These illusions use the way your brain processes optical information to fool you into seeing things that are not there.

Examining how people react to optical illusions will help you understand how the eyes and brain work. In this set of experiments, you will explore how people perceive images. For each of the images illustrated on the following pages, write a hypothesis about what people will see. For example, for the second picture, you will ask ten people this question: "Which figure is larger?" How do you think people will answer?

Before you begin, make an educated guess about the outcome of this experiment based on your knowledge of how your brain perceives images. This educated guess, or prediction, is your **hypothesis.** A hypothesis should explain these things:

What Are the Variables?

Variables are anything that might affect the results of an experiment. Here are the main variables in this experiment:

- the image you are testing
- the people you use as test subjects
- the different ways the image can be seen
- the lighting on the image
- what you tell the test subject about the image before he or she views it

In other words, the variables in this experiment are everything that might affect how a person perceives the image. If you change more than one variable, you will not be able to tell which variable had the most effect on the test subject's perception.

What do you see?

Which figure is larger?

LEFT: Optical illusion #1.

RIGHT: Optical illusion #2.

- the topic of the experiment
- the variable you will change
- the variable you will measure
- what you expect to happen

A hypothesis should be brief, specific, and measurable. It must be something you can test through observation. Your experiment will prove or disprove your hypothesis. Here is one possible hypothesis for the first image in this experiment: "Eight out of ten people will see non-parallel lines." Write a hypothesis for the other images.

In this case, the **variable** you will change will be the person viewing the image, and the variable you will measure will be how that person perceives the image. For the first image, you expect that most, but not all, of the people will perceive that the lines are not parallel.

Remember, the more people you test, the more accurate your results will be. After you complete these experiments, you will draw some conclusions about how the mind perceives visual images.

Level of Difficulty
Difficult because of the need to gather test subjects.

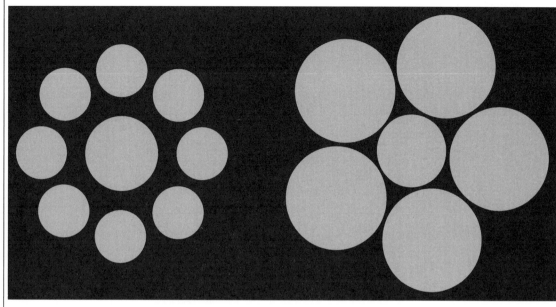

Which inner circle is larger?

Materials Needed

- images provided throughout Experiment 2
- at least 10 people as test subjects
- paper and pencil
- a well-lighted room

Approximate Budget

$0.

Timetable

Depends on the subjects' availability.

Step-by-Step Instructions

1. Find at least ten people who are willing to participate in your project. Explain the task to them.

2. Photocopy the images illustrated throughout Experiment 2, enlarging them, if possible. Make sure the copies are clear.

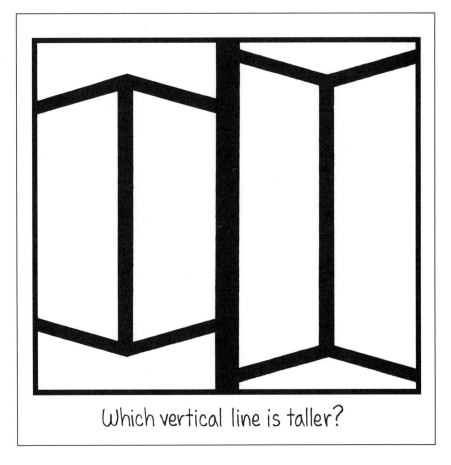

Which vertical line is taller?

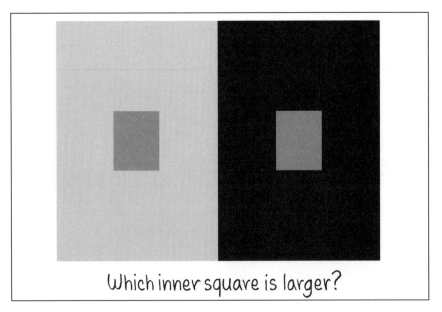

Which inner square is larger?

experiment
CENTRAL

How to Experiment Safely

There are no hazards associated with this experiment.

3. Prepare a question for each of the images.

4. List the images on a data sheet, number them, and record the question you will ask for each one. Make a column where you will write each subject's answer.

   Make a copy of the data sheet for each subject.

5. Conduct your interviews with one subject at a time. Carefully record their answers on a data sheet.

Troubleshooter's Guide

Experiments using people can be difficult. Here are some problems that may arise during this experiment, some possible causes, and ways to remedy the problems.

Problem: Subjects look at images for a long time and say they can see it in many ways.

Possible cause: Explain clearly that you are trying to explore the way perception works and so you want their first reaction. Tell them not to spend too much time analyzing what they see.

Problem: It is difficult to draw conclusions from the many different answers subjects gave.

Possible cause: Everyone perceives things a little differently. Study how your subjects responded, think about what you see, and try to think of reasons why people may see things differently. Do you think it has to do with their eyes? Their brains? Their past experience? You may decide that you cannot draw any conclusions from the data you collected. That often happens in the field of science.

Summary of Results

Study your findings carefully. Did people have similar reactions to the images, or were they varied? What conclusions, if any, can you draw about the way the eyes and the brain work together on perception? Were any or all of your hypotheses correct?

Change the Variables

You can vary this experiment in several ways. For example, locate other optical illusions and test people's reactions. How does this add to what you learned about perception in the first set of experiments? Does it change your ideas, or confirm them? Or you can try testing a different set of people. Ask young children, older people, or another group. Do their responses change? Can you draw any conclusions about the way people perceive things as they get older?

 **Design Your Own Experiment**

How to Select a Topic Relating to this Concept

If you are interested in optics, you could further investigate kinds of lenses. You could examine reflection and refraction with mirrors or prisms, which bend light and separate out the different wavelengths so you can see different colors. You could study the effects of polarizers, which line up different wavelengths of light, creating interesting effects, like the polarizing filters used on cameras.

If you are interested in optical instruments, you can build your own camera or investigate telescopes, microscopes, and magnifying lenses. You can explore illusions involving color, movement, and three-dimensional objects. Or you could explore the work of M.C. Escher, who drew pictures that confuse the mind.

Check the For More Information section and talk with your science teacher or school or community media specialist to start gathering information on optics questions that interest you.

Steps in the Scientific Method

To do an original experiment, you need to plan carefully and think things through. Otherwise you might not be sure what question you are answering, what you are or should be measuring, or what your findings prove or disprove.

Example of a M.C. Escher drawing: these stairs appear to go nowhere. (Art Resource. Reproduced by permission.)

Here are the steps in designing an experiment:

- State the purpose of—and underlying question behind—the experiment you propose to do.
- Recognize the variables involved, and select one that will help you answer the question at hand.
- State a testable hypothesis, an educated guess about the answer to your question.
- Decide how to change the variable you selected.
- Decide how to measure your results.

Recording Data and Summarizing the Results

Your data should include charts, such as the ones you did in these experiments, that are clearly labeled and easy to read. You may also want to include photos, graphs, or drawings of your experimental set-up and results.

If you are preparing an exhibit for a science fair, display any optical instruments you built or copies of the illusions you worked with. If you have done a nonexperimental project, explain clearly what your research question was and illustrate your findings.

Related Projects

There are also other ways you can explore the topic of optics, such as building models of optical instruments or studying their history.

If you are interested in perception, you could explore the connections between perception and art and research artists who have studied how the mind perceives images. All of these ideas would lead to fascinating projects.

For More Information

Ardley, Neil. *Science Book of Light.* Burlington, MA: Harcourt Brace, 1991. ❖ Simple experiments demonstrating principles of light.

Armstrong, Tim. *Make Moving Patterns: How to Make Optical Illusions of Your Own.* Jersey City, NJ: Parkwest Publications, 1993. ❖ Ideas for creating your own series of optical illusions.

Levine, Shar, Leslie Johnstone, and Jason Coons. *The Optics Book: Fun Experiments with Light, Vision & Color.* New York: Sterling Publications, 1998. ❖ Informative book on light, vision, and optical instruments, with experiments, explanations, and drawings.

chapter 30

Osmosis and Diffusion

Gas and liquid **molecules** are always in motion. They move randomly in all directions and bounce around and into each other. As they move, molecules have a tendency to spread out, moving from areas with many molecules to areas with fewer molecules. This process of spreading out is called **diffusion.**

You have probably noticed diffusion in your home. If you opened a bottle of vanilla in your kitchen, for example, you probably could soon smell the vanilla in all parts of the room. The vanilla spread through the air from an area of high **concentration** of vanilla molecules to areas of less concentration. They diffused throughout the room—and perhaps throughout the house.

Osmosis (pronounced oz-MO-sis) is a kind of diffusion. Osmosis occurs when a substance diffuses across a **semiperme-**

The smell of vanilla quickly diffuses in all directions. (Grant Heilman. Reproduced by permission.)

Words to Know

Concentration:
The amount of a substance present in a given volume, such as the number of molecules in a liter.

Control experiment:
A set-up that is identical to the experiment but is not affected by the variable that will be changed during the experiment.

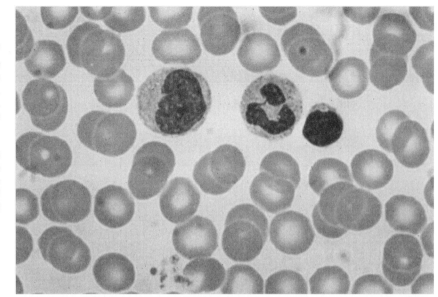

TOP: Oxygen enters blood cells by diffusing from areas of high concentration to areas of low concentration. (Photo Researchers Inc. Reproduced by permission.)

BOTTOM: A helium balloon is a semipermeable membrane. (Photo Researchers Inc. Reproduced by permission.)

ⓦords to Know

Diffusion:
Random movement of molecules that leads to a net movement of molecules from a region of high concentration to a region of low concentration.

Dynamic equilibrium:
A situation in which substances are moving into and out of cell walls at an equal rate.

Hypertonic solution:
A solution with a higher concentration of materials than a cell immersed in the solution.

Hypothesis:
An idea in the form of a statement that can be tested by observation and/or experiment.

Hypotonic solution:
A solution with a lower concentration of materials than a cell immersed in the solution.

able membrane from an area of high concentration to an area of low concentration. A semipermeable membrane lets some substances through but not others.

What are some examples of diffusion?

Diffusion takes place constantly in our bodies and is vital to cell functioning. Cell walls are selectively permeable, meaning that certain substances can pass through them, but others cannot. Diffusion allows certain materials to move into and out of cell walls, from a higher concentration to a lower concentration.

For example, oxygen diffuses from the air sacs in your lungs into your blood capillaries because the concentration of oxygen is higher in the air sacs and lower in the capillary blood.

Different kinds of membranes allow differing amounts of diffusion to occur. Think about a helium balloon. It starts out full of helium and floats upwards, but over a period of a day or two it loses helium until it is no longer lighter than air and cannot float any more. Why does this happen? The balloon allows the helium atoms to pass through it into the atmosphere. Helium atoms slowly diffuse from an area of high concentration (inside the balloon) to an area of lesser concentration (the great outdoors).

How does osmosis work?

When materials move into and out of a cell at equal rates, the cell is said to be balanced, or in **dynamic equilibrium.** An **isotonic solution** has a concentration of materials the same as that inside a cell. If a cell is placed in an isotonic solution, molecules will still move into and out of the cell, but the cell will be in dynamic equilibrium. If a substance is in lower concentration outside a cell than inside the cell, the substance will leave the cell through osmosis. Likewise, the substance will move into the cell if the situation is reversed.

A **hypotonic solution,** where the concentration of substances is lower than that in the cell, draws substances out of the cell. What do you think will happen if the cell is in a **hypertonic solution,** where the concentration of materials in the solution is higher than that inside the cell?

We see examples of osmosis and diffusion all around us. When you add water to a wilted plant, for example, it soon stands up straight. You have just seen osmosis in action! Do you have questions of your own about osmosis? You will have an opportunity to explore osmosis and diffusion in the following experiments.

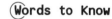
Words to Know

Isotonic solutions:
Two solutions that have the same concentration of solute particles and therefore the same osmotic pressure.

Molecule:
The smallest particle of a substance that retains all the properties of the substance and is composed of one or more atoms.

Osmosis:
The movement of fluids and substances dissolved in liquids across a semipermeable membrane from an area of its greater concentration to an area of its lesser concentration until all substances involved reach a balance.

Semipermeable membrane:
A thin barrier between two solutions that permits only certain components of the solutions, usually the solvent, to pass through.

Variable:
Something that can affect the results of an experiment.

Experiment 1
Measuring Membranes: Is a plastic bag a semipermeable membrane?

Purpose/Hypothesis

In this experiment, you will find out how a thin plastic bag functions as a membrane. If it is semipermeable, it will allow some kinds of molecules to pass through but not others. For example, the plastic might allow small molecules to pass through, but not larger ones. You will test two solutions—iodine and starch, each with a different size molecule—to see what happens. Before you begin, make an educated guess about the outcome of this experiment based on your knowledge of osmosis. This educated guess, or prediction, is your **hypothesis.** A hypothesis should explain these things:

- the topic of the experiment
- the variable you will change
- the variable you will measure
- what you expect to happen

A hypothesis should be brief, specific, and measurable. It must be something you can test through observation. Your experiment will prove or disprove your hypothesis. Here is one possible hypothesis for this experiment: "Iodine will cross through the plastic membrane, while starch will not."

In this case, the **variable** you will change will be the solutions. The variable you will measure will be changes in the solutions in the bag and in the measuring cup that holds the bag. You expect the iodine solution to pass through the plastic baggie, while the starch solution will not.

Setting up a **control experiment** will help you isolate one variable. Only one variable will change between the control and the experimental set-up, and that is the solution in the plastic bag. For the control, you will use a bag of water. For your experiment, you will use a bag of starch solution. You will put both bags into iodine solutions in measuring cups.

After you allow the solutions time to diffuse through the bag, you will observe the color and the volume of water in both the plastic bags and the measuring cups. A color change may occur because when

What Are the Variables?

Variables are anything that might affect the results of an experiment. Here are the main variables in this experiment:

- the kind of solution
- the kind of membrane
- the thickness of the membrane
- the temperature of the solutions
- the color of the solutions
- the volume of the solution inside the bag and in the measuring cup

In other words, the variables in this experiment are everything that might affect whether a solution passes through a membrane. If you change more than one variable, you will not be able to tell which variable had the most effect on the passage of the solution through the membrane.

iodine comes into contact with starch, the starch solution turns bluish-black. If the starch solution in the bag turns bluish-black, you will know that iodine solution in the measuring cup has crossed through the plastic membrane and entered the bag. If the blue iodine solution in the measuring cup turns black, you will know that starch has crossed through the membrane into the cup. If the solution in the bag turns black, but the cup solution does not, you know your hypothesis is correct: iodine crossed through the plastic membrane, but the starch did not.

Level of Difficulty
Moderate.

Materials Needed
- 2 quart-size (1-liter size) measuring cups
- a smaller measuring cup or graduated cylinder
- small sealable plastic bags
- cornstarch
- water

How to Experiment Safely

Wash your hands before, during, and after the experiment, so you do not transfer the starch or iodine on your hands. Wear goggles so you do not get the iodine in your eyes. Be careful with all glassware.

- iodine with dropper
- masking tape
- measuring spoons and cups
- goggles

Approximate Budget

Less than $10. (Most of these materials should be available in the average household.)

Timetable

2 days, leaving experiments overnight.

Step-by-Step Instructions

1. Prepare your solutions. Add 1 tablespoon (15 milliliters) of cornstarch for each cup of water to make the starch solution. Add 10 drops of iodine for each cup of water to make the iodine solution. You will probably need a total of 10 to 12 cups of each solution.

2. For your control, fill one baggie with water. Seal it tightly to prevent leakage. Place 2 to 3 cups iodine solution in one large measuring cup. Record the exact

Step 3: Water baggie in the measuring cup.

amount of solution in the cup, using the measuring lines on the side of the cup.

3. Fill another measuring cup with 2 cups (500 milliliters) of plain water. Place the water baggie in this cup and record how much the water level rises. The difference in the water level is the volume of the water in your baggie.

TOP: Steps 7 and 8: "Control" and "Experiment" measuring cups.

BOTTOM: Step 9: Data chart for Experiment 1.

Data Chart

	Control (iodine/water)	Experiment (iodine/starch)
Start Volume		
End Volume		
Start color in Bag		
End color in Bag		

4. Place the water baggie in the cup of iodine solution you prepared. Label the cup "control" with masking tape and set it aside.

5. Fill another baggie with starch solution and seal it. Measure and record its volume, as in Step 3. Carefully rinse the outside of the bag with water to wash off any starch solution.

6. Place 2 cups (500 milliliters) of iodine solution in another large measuring cup. Record the exact volume.

7. Lower the bag of starch solution into the iodine solution. Label this cup "experiment."

8. Let the control and experimental cups sit overnight.

9. The next day, check the solutions in the bags and in the cups. What colors are they? Measure and record the volume of water in the cups and the bags.

 ## Troubleshooter's Guide

Experiments do not always work out as planned. Even so, figuring out what went wrong can be a learning experience. Here are some problems that may arise during this experiment, some possible causes, and ways to remedy the problems.

Problem: The iodine solution changed color right away.

Possible cause: Starch solution leaked out or was on the outside of the bag. Seal your bag tighter and wash the outside carefully.

Problem: There was no change in color.

Possible cause: Those plastic baggies are not permeable to either solution. Try a thinner baggie or a different brand.

Problem: There is no change in volume.

Possible cause: The solutions are not strong enough. Try adding more cornstarch or iodine to your solutions.

Summary of Results

Study the results on your chart. Did the color of the solutions change? Remember that if the starch solution in the bag turned black, iodine entered through the plastic membrane. If the iodine solution in the cup turned black, starch must have leaked out of the bag. If the volume of solution in the bag increased, you know that molecules were entering the bag, but few were leaving. Was your hypothesis correct? What have you discovered? What happened in the control cup?

Change the Variables

You can change the variables and repeat this experiment. For example, try adding more iodine and cornstarch to create stronger solutions. See how that affects the change in volume and/or the rate of osmosis. (Or try using weaker solutions.) You can also try using different varieties of plastic bags or different materials altogether. See which ones allow certain solutions through and how quickly.

Experiment 2
Changing Concentrations: Will a bag of salt water draw in fresh water?

Purpose/Hypothesis

In this experiment, you will see osmosis in action. You will place a balloon filled with salt water into a bucket of fresh water and watch what happens. Before you begin, make an educated guess about the outcome of this experiment based on your knowledge of osmosis. This educated guess, or prediction, is your **hypothesis.** A hypothesis should explain these things:

- the topic of the experiment
- the variable you will change
- the variable you will measure
- what you expect to happen

A hypothesis should be brief, specific, and measurable. It must be something you can test through observation. Your experiment will prove or disprove your hypothesis. Here is one possible hypothesis for this experiment: "A balloon filled with salt water will expand when placed in fresh water."

What Are the Variables?

Variables are anything that might affect the results of an experiment. Here are the main variables in this experiment:

- type of solution in balloon
- thickness of balloon
- the temperature of the water
- amount of water in the bucket and the balloon

In other words, the variables in this experiment are everything that might affect the movement of water across the membrane. If you change more than one variable, you will not be able to tell which variable had the most effect on the movement across the membrane.

In this case, the **variable** you will change will be the kind of water you put in the balloon and the variable you will measure will be how much water enters the balloon as reflected by changes in the volume of the balloon. You expect the balloon filled with salt water will absorb fresh water and expand.

Only one variable will change between the **control experiment** and the experimental balloon, and that is the kind of solution inside the balloon. For the control, you will use fresh water. For your experimental balloons, you will use two different concentrations of salt water. You will measure how much water is in the balloons after they soak in fresh water. If the experimental balloons gain water when they have salt water in them, and the control balloon does not, then your hypothesis will be supported.

Level of Difficulty

Easy.

Materials Needed

- salt
- at least three thin balloons or sealable baggies
- 3 buckets or other large containers
- funnel

How to Experiment Safely
There are no safety hazards in this experiment.

- measuring cup
- measuring spoons
- 2 bowls
- stirrer

Approximate Budget
$3 for balloons.

Timetable
1 hour to set up the experiment; 1 day to view the results.

Step-by-Step Instructions
1. Measure 12 cups (6 pints or 2.8 liters) of water into each bucket.

2. Use the funnel to pour 1 cup (.5 liter) of fresh water into a balloon. Tie the balloon tightly and place it in a bucket labeled "control."

3. Use the bowls to prepare two salt solutions with different concentrations. For Solution 1, add 3 teaspoons of salt to 2 cups of water. For Solution 2, add 9 teaspoons of salt to another 2 cups of water. Stir both solutions until the salt dissolves.

4. Use the funnel to pour one cup of Solution 1 into one balloon and

Step 2: Funneling fresh water into a balloon.

experiment
CENTRAL

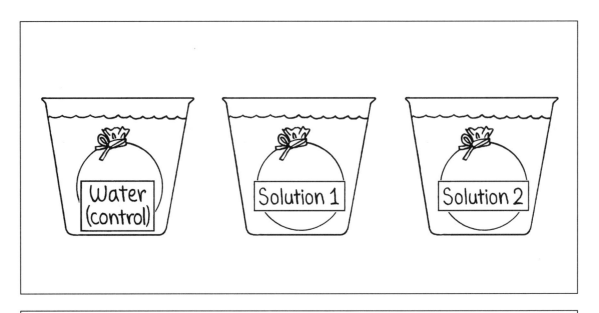

Data Chart

	Control Balloon	Solution 1 Balloon	Solution 2 Balloon
Start Volume			
End Volume			

TOP: Steps 2 to 5: Balloons in labeled buckets.

BOTTOM: Step 7: Data chart for Experiment 2.

tie it tightly. Rinse the funnel. Then use the funnel to pour one cup of Solution 2 into another balloon and tie it tightly.

5. Place each balloon into its own bucket, labeled "Solution 1" and "Solution 2."

6. Leave all three buckets overnight.

7. The next day, examine all three balloons. Measure the change in volume by placing each one in a large (1000-milliliter) measuring

Troubleshooter's Guide

Here are some problems that may arise during this experiment, some possible causes, and ways to remedy the problems.

Problem: No volume change occurred at all.

Possible causes:

1. You have used a very thick balloon that is not permeable. Try a different kind of balloon or baggie.

2. Your solutions were not well mixed. Try adding more salt and stirring longer.

Problem: One or more of the balloons exploded.

Possible cause: The balloon membrane is very thin and too much water entered. Try using weaker salt solutions or not leaving the balloon in the water for as long.

cup filled with 2 cups (500 milliliters) of water. Record how high the water rises. The difference is the volume in the balloon.

Summary of Results

Study the results on your chart. Compare the change in volume for each balloon to any change in your control. The more volume the balloons gained, the greater amount of osmosis occurred. What did you find? Was your hypothesis correct? Write a paragraph summarizing and explaining your findings.

Change the Variables

There are several ways you can vary this experiment. For example, try other salt concentrations. Add more salt or less. Or try sugar or starch solutions and see what effect those have on amount of osmosis that occurs. You can also experiment with different membranes, such as thicker or thinner balloons or baggies or balloons made of Mylar. See what kind of effect these have on osmosis. Finally, you can see how long osmosis takes under the different conditions you are testing.

experiment
CENTRAL

 **Design Your Own Experiment**

How to Select a Topic Relating to this Concept

If you are interested in osmosis and diffusion, you might study their effects on living organisms or the effects of different solutions on plants or on simple one-celled organisms, such as a paramecium.

Are you interested in rates of diffusion? Try timing how long different solutions take to diffuse throughout water. Or create solutions using different-size molecules and higher and lower concentrations. You might separate solutions and then watch what diffuses through membranes.

Check the For More Information section and talk with your science teacher or school or community media specialist to start gathering information on osmosis questions that interest you.

Steps in the Scientific Method

To do an original experiment, you need to plan carefully and think things through. Otherwise you might not be sure what question you are answering, what you are or should be measuring, or what your findings prove or disprove.

Here are the steps in designing an experiment:

- State the purpose of—and underlying question behind—the experiment you propose to do.
- Recognize the variables involved, and select one that will help you answer the question at hand.
- State a testable hypothesis, an educated guess about the answer to your question.
- Decide how to change the variable you selected.
- Decide how to measure your results.

Recording Data and Summarizing the Results

Your data should include charts, such as the ones you did in these experiments. All charts should be clearly labeled and easy to read. You may also want to include photos, graphs, or drawings of your experimental set-up and results.

If you are preparing an exhibit for a science fair, display your results, such as any experimental set-ups you built. If you have done a nonexperimental project, explain clearly what your research question was and illustrate your findings.

Related Projects

You can design projects that are similar to these experiments, involving trials and charts of data to summarize your results. You could also prepare a model that demonstrates a point you are interested in with regard to osmosis or diffusion. Or you could investigate the effects of osmosis in a certain environment. There are many options.

For More Information

Gardner, Robert. *Experimenting with Water.* New York: Franklin Watts, 1993. ❖ Fascinating experiments that explore the strange properties of water.

Vancleave, Janice Pratt. *Janice Vancleave's Biology for Every Kid: One Hundred One Easy Experiments That Really Work.* New York: John Wiley & Sons, 1989. ❖ Basic principles of biology of plants and animals through informative text and experiments.

experiment
CENTRAL

chapter 31

Oxidation-Reduction

Do you know what rusting metal, photographic processes, battery operation, and clothes bleaching have in common? They are all examples of an important and common kind of chemical reaction called an **oxidation-reduction reaction.** This kind of reaction involves the transfer of **electrons,** which are tiny particles in **atoms.** During **oxidation,** a substance's atoms lose electrons. During **reduction,** a substance's atoms gain electrons.

What actually happens during oxidation?

To understand oxidation, it is important to understand how atoms work. All atoms have three kinds of tiny particles—electrons, **protons,** and **neutrons.** Electrons have negative electrical charges, while protons have positive charges. Neutrons are neutral—neither positive nor negative. The sum of the electrical charges in each atom is balanced, so atoms are electrically neutral.

The **oxidation state** of an atom is the sum of its positive and negative charges, and the oxidation state of any atom is zero. Oxidation reactions involve a change in the oxidation state of the atoms involved, caused by a loss or gain of electrons.

During oxidation, an atom loses electrons and becomes a positively charged **ion.** (An ion is an atom or a group of atoms that carries an electrical charge, either positive or negative.) Metal atoms tend to undergo oxidation easily. In an oxidation reaction, the metal loses one, two, or three electrons and becomes positively charged. The other substance, a nonmetal, gains electrons, becoming a negatively charged

Words to Know

Atom:
The smallest unit of an element, made up of protons and neutrons in a central nucleus surrounded by moving electrons.

Control Experiment:
A set-up that is identical to the experiment but is not affected by the variable that affects the experimental group. Results from the control experiment are compared to results from the actual experiment.

TOP: Rust destroys millions of dollars in property every year. (Photo Researchers Inc. Reproduced by permission.)

BOTTOM: Batteries work by an oxidation/reduction reaction. (Photo Researchers Inc. Reproduced by permission.)

Words to Know

Corrosion:
An oxidation-reduction reaction in which a metal is oxidized (reacted with oxygen) and oxygen is reduced, usually in the presence of moisture.

Electron:
A subatomic particle with a mass of about one atomic mass unit and a single negative electrical charge that orbits the nucleus of an atom.

Hypothesis:
An idea in the form of a statement that can be tested by observation and/or experiment

Ion:
An atom or groups of atoms that carries an electrical charge—either positive or negative—as a result of losing or gaining one or more electrons.

ion. The nonmetal is thus reduced. Remember that oxidation cannot occur without a corresponding reduction reaction.

What are some examples of oxidation?

One common example of an oxidation reaction is the one that occurs between sodium, a soft metal, and chlorine, a gas. When these elements exchange one electron, a violent reaction occurs, and a new substance, sodium chloride, is formed. We know it as the hard, white substance often found on the kitchen table: salt.

Here is what happens: both sodium (Na) and chlorine gas (Cl_2) are electrically neutral. When they combine, sodium undergoes oxidation, loses an electron, and becomes positively charged. Chlorine undergoes reduction and becomes negatively charged. Because atoms do not "like" to be charged, the sodium and the chlorine are attracted to their opposite charges and combine to create salt.

Oxidation reactions play an important role in many processes of modern life; the results are all around us. One of the most common places you see the results of oxidation is in the process of **corrosion**, particularly involving iron and steel. Iron oxide flakes off in what we call rust.

An **oxidizing agent** is anything that causes another substance to lose electrons. Bleaches are one example. Bleaches remove electrons that are activated by light to produce colors.

What kind of questions do you have about oxidation-reduction? You'll have an opportunity to explore oxidation in the following experiments and think about designing your own experiments on this important and far-reaching topic.

Experiment 1
Reduction: How will acid affect dirty pennies?

Purpose/Hypothesis
In this experiment, you will find out how an acid leads to a reducing reaction, and you will explore the movement of atoms during the reaction. Acids are important reducing agents, involved in many common chemical reactions in our daily lives.

Pennies are coated with copper oxide (CuO), which forms when copper combines with oxygen from the air. Pennies look dirty when they are coated copper oxide. In this experiment, you will immerse pennies into a mixture of vinegar or lemon juice and salt—which dissolves copper oxide. (Vinegar and lemon juice are weak acids; the salt helps the reaction.) When you put the dirty pennies into the solution, the copper oxide and copper will dissolve into the water. Some of the copper atoms

Neutron:
A subatomic particle with a mass of about one atomic mass unit and no electrical charge that is found in the nucleus of an atom.

Oxidation:
A chemical reaction in which oxygen reacts with some other substance and in which ions, atoms, or molecules lose electrons.

Oxidation-reduction reaction:
A chemical reaction in which one substance loses one or more electrons and the other substance gains one or more electrons.

Oxidation state:
The sum of an atom's positive and negative charges.

Oxidizing agent:
A chemical substance that gives up oxygen or takes on electrons from another substance.

will leave their electrons behind and float in the water as positively charged copper ions, missing two electrons. They have been reduced.

When you put steel nails into the same solution, the salt and vinegar dissolve some of the iron from the nails. When the iron atoms leave, they also leave electrons behind just as the copper did. Now you will have positively charged iron ions floating around in the solution with the positively charged copper ions. Since the nails will now have extra electrons left on them from the iron atoms that dissolved into the solution, the nails are negatively charged. What happens when there are positive and negative charges near each other? They attract! What do you think will happen to the copper ions as they get near the negatively charged nails?

Do you have an educated guess about what will happen to the pennies and the nails in the acidic solution? That educated guess, or prediction, is your hypothesis. A **hypothesis** should explain these things:

- the topic of the experiment
- the **variable** you will change
- the variable you will measure
- what you expect to happen

A hypothesis should be brief, specific, and measurable. It must be something you can test through observation. Your experiment will prove or disprove your hypothesis. Here is one possible hypothesis for this experiment: "An acidic solution will cause the pennies to become clean and copper to coat the nails."

Variables are anything that can be changed in an experiment. In this case, the variable you will change will be the acid in your solution, and the variable you will measure will be the color (a measure of cleanliness) of the pennies and the color of the nails after they have soaked in the solution.

Setting up a **control experiment** will help you isolate one variable. Only one variable will change between the control and the experimental bowls, and that variable is the kind of solution you use to immerse the pennies and nails. For the control, you will use plain water. For your experimental bowls, you will use lemon juice and vinegar.

You will record the color of the pennies and the nails both before and after you immerse them in the solutions. If the pennies become

Words to Know

Proton:
A subatomic particle with a mass of about one atomic mass unit and a single positive electrical charge that is found in the nucleus of an atom.

Reduction:
A process in which a chemical substance gives off oxygen or takes on electrons.

Variable:
Something that may affect the results of an experiment.

 What Are the Variables?

Variables are anything that might affect the results of an experiment. Here are the main variables in this experiment:

- the kind of solution being used

- the cleanliness of the pennies prior to the experiment

- the time allowed for the pennies and nails to soak in the solution

- the color of the pennies and the nails after they have soaked in the solution

In order to test your hypothesis, you can change only one variable at a time. If you change more than one, you will not be able to tell which factor caused a change in the outcome of your experiment.

cleaner and brighter, and the nails become copper-colored, your hypothesis is supported.

Level of difficulty
Moderate.

Materials Needed
- 45 equally dirty pennies
- 1/4 cup lemon juice
- 1/4 cup white vinegar
- 1/4 cup water
- 2 teaspoons salt
- 3 glass or ceramic bowls
- 6 clean steel nails (not galvanized nails)
- paper towels
- goggles
- rubber gloves

Approximate Budget
Up to $5. (Try to borrow the goggles from your school.)

Timetable
2 hours.

How to Experiment Safely

Wash your hands before and after handling the dirty pennies and other materials. Wear goggles and rubber gloves to avoid eye and skin contact with the acid solutions. Be careful in handling the nails to avoid cuts or punctures.

Step-by-Step Instructions

1. Put water in one bowl, lemon juice in another, and vinegar in a third. Label each bowl if you need help telling them apart.

2. Add 1 teaspoon salt to the vinegar solution and to the lemon juice, and stir until it dissolves.

3. Examine the color of the pennies carefully. Describe the color on your data sheet, illustrated.

4. Place one penny in each bowl. Describe what happens on your data sheet.

5. Place 14 more pennies in each bowl. Watch what happens to them.

6. After 5 minutes, remove the pennies from one bowl. Rinse them thoroughly under running water and place them on a paper towel

Steps 1 to 5: Bowl set-up with pennies.

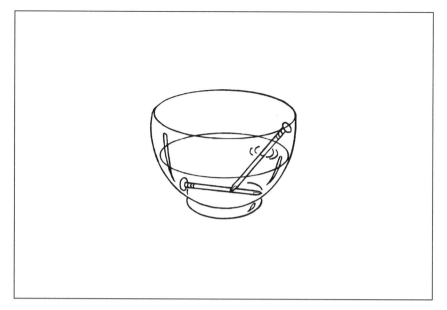

Step 9: Place a nail in each bowl. Lean a second nail against the side of the bowl so only about half of it is in the solution.

to dry. Write the kind of solution they were soaking in on the paper towel.

7. Repeat Step 6 with the pennies from the other two bowls.

8. Examine the nails carefully and describe their color on your data sheet.

9. Place a nail in each bowl. Lean a second nail against the side of the bowl so only about half of it is in the solution.

Step 3: Data sheet for Experiment 1.

Solution	Penny color before	Penny color after	Nail color after 10 minutes	Nail color after one hour

10. After 10 minutes, examine the nails. Record the colors on your data sheet.

11. Leave the nails for an hour and then examine them again.

Summary of Results
Study the results on your chart. What have you discovered? What color changes took place? Why? Was your hypothesis correct? Write a paragraph to summarize and explain your findings.

Change the Variables
You can vary this experiment. Here are some possibilities:

• Try different solutions to see how they affect the oxidation/reduction reaction, such as baking soda, bleach, or tomato juice. Or try

Troubleshooter's Guide
Below are some problems that may occur during the experiment, possible causes, and ways to remedy the problems.

Problem: The pennies did not change color in any of the solutions.

Possible causes:

1. Your pennies were not dirty enough. Find dirtier pennies and repeat the experiment.

2. Your solutions are not acidic enough. Check the expiration dates on your bottles of vinegar and lemon juice, and replace them, if necessary.

Problem: The nails did not pick up any copper at all.

Possible causes:

1. Make sure your nails are steel and clean. Impurities can affect the oxidation reaction.

2. You may not have left them in solution long enough, or if the pennies did not have much copper oxide on them, little copper will be in solution. Run the experiment again with dirtier pennies and leave the nails for a longer time.

diluting the solutions with water to vary the ratio of water to acid. Be sure to record how much of each you use. Again, be careful in handling these liquids. Wear goggles and gloves and work in a ventilated area, especially when using bleach.

- Vary the time you leave the pennies and nails in the solution. What happens?

Experiment 2
Oxidation and Rust: How is rust produced?

Purpose/Hypothesis

One of the most common oxidation reactions is the production of rust, otherwise known as corrosion. Iron readily combines with water and oxygen to form rust.

In this experiment, you will explore the process of iron oxidation, which produces rust. You will see the result of the depletion of oxygen as this element is removed from the air to combine with iron.

Do you have an educated guess about how water will affect a piece of steel wool? What might happen to a candle burning in the same container as the steel wool? That educated guess, or prediction, is your hypothesis. A **hypothesis** should explain these things:

- the topic of the experiment
- the **variable** you will change
- the variable you will measure
- what you expect to happen

A hypothesis should be brief, specific, and measurable. It must be something you can test through observation. Your experi-

You can see rust on metal fences all over the world. (Peter Arnold Inc. Reproduced by permission.)

What Are the Variables?

Variables are anything that could affect the results of an experiment. Here are the variables in this experiment:

- the amount of water in jars
- the amount of air in each jar
- the material used in water
- the type of steel wool
- the type of candles
- the time the candles burn after the steel wool is removed

In order to test your hypothesis, you can change only one variable at a time. If you change more than one, you will not be able to tell which factor caused a change in the outcome of your experiment.

ment will prove or disprove your hypothesis. Here is one possible hypothesis for this experiment: "Wet steel wool will oxidize to form rust when left for several days. This process removes oxygen from the air, so a candle placed in the same space will burn for a shorter amount of time."

In this case, the variable you will change will be whether the steel wool is exposed to water. The variable you will measure will be the amount of rust on the steel wool and the length of time the candle burns.

Setting up a control experiment will help you isolate one variable. Only one variable will change between the control and the experimental jar, and that is whether the steel wool is exposed to moisture. For the control, you will use dry steel wool. For your experimental jar, you will use damp steel wool.

You will measure how much oxidation or rust occurs and how long the candles burn. If the control shows no rust while your experimental jar shows some, AND the candle burns for a shorter amount of time in the experimental jar, your hypothesis is supported.

Level of Difficulty

Easy/moderate; ask an adult to help you light the candles.

Materials Needed

- 2 equal-sized pieces of steel wool (Do not use scouring pads that contain soap.)
- 2 identical glass jars with metal lids
- water
- 2 small birthday candles
- matches
- a small amount of modeling clay
- stopwatch

Approximate Budget

$5 to $7 if you need to purchase steel wool, modeling clay and/or candles.

Timetable

3 days.

Step-by-Step Instructions

1. Wet one piece of steel wool and place it in one of the jars. In the other jar, place a dry piece of steel wool. Label each jar carefully.

2. Close both lids tightly and place the jars in a cool, dark place for three days.

3. Have an adult light one of the candles.

4. Open the experimental jar and have the adult drop in the candle. Quickly close the jar again.

How to Experiment Safely

Be careful handling glass jars to avoid breakage. As with all fire, be extremely careful handling matches. You are strongly urged to have an adult help you light the candles. Have water or a fire extinguisher close by in case of an accident.

Step 1: Set-up of "wet" and "dry" jars.

wet steel wool →   wet   dry   ← dry steel wool

Steps 3 and 4: Dropping lit candle into experimental jar.

wet steel wool →   wet

5. Use the stopwatch to time how long the candle burns. Record the time on a chart like the one illustrated.

6. Repeat Steps 3 to 5, having your adult helper drop the other lighted candle in the control jar.

7. After both candles have burned, remove the steel wool from both jars and record what you find.

	Rust?	Candle burning time
Dry steel wool		
Wet steel wool		

Summary of Results

Study your results, comparing the amounts of rust on each piece of steel wool and the times the two candles burned. The more rust you

Data chart for Experiment 2.

Troubleshooter's Guide

Below are some problems that may occur during this experiment, possible causes, and ways to remedy the problems.

Problem: No rust showed on the either piece of steel wool.

Possible cause: You did not put enough water on the experimental steel wool. Try wetting it more, or putting a small amount of water in the base of the jar before leaving it.

Possible cause: You did not leave the jars long enough. Try leaving both jars for several more days.

Problem: The candles burned the same length of time.

Possible cause: You let in too much outside air when you opened the jars. Open and close the jars as quickly as possible so little outside air will have an opportunity to mix with the air in the jars.

observe, the more oxidation occurred. The shorter time the candles burned, the less oxygen was present in the jars, showing that more oxidation occurred. What did you discover? Was your hypothesis supported? Write a paragraph summarizing and explaining your results.

Change the Variables

You can vary this experiment. Here are some possibilities:

- Try using other kinds of metal, such as screws and nails, tinfoil, painted steel wool, or even different brands of steel wool, to see what oxidizes more readily. See if you can isolate factors that cause more rust than others, such as the amount of exposed surface area or the shape, size, or color of the metal.
- See what happens when you leave the experimental set-up for several more days. How much more rust do you find? Can you make any additional predictions about the effect of oxidation on other objects?

 # Design Your Own Experiment

How to Select a Topic Relating to this Concept

Oxidation-reduction reactions take place all around you every day. Are you interested in corrosion of metals? Try experimenting with different kinds of metals to see which ones corrode faster and what happens to them when they corrode. Or investigate bleaching action, involving electrons activated by light. Another reaction involving light is that of photo-chromic glass, which causes eyeglasses to darken in direct sunlight because of photo-oxidation.

Perhaps you are interested in how batteries work. Most of them involve oxidation-reduction reactions with various compounds such as ammonium chloride, silver oxide, mercury, or nickel/cadmium. If you experiment with batteries, use extreme caution because they contain potentially toxic compounds.

Oxidation-reduction reactions are involved in photosynthesis, metabolism, nitrogen fixation, fuel combustion, and many other things. The possibilities for investigation are endless. Think about your interests and check the For More Information section. Talk with your teachers or librarians about how you can get further information on the topics that interest you.

Steps in the Scientific Method

To do an original experiment, you need to plan carefully and think things through before you do it. Otherwise you might not be sure what question you are answering, what you are or should be measuring, or what your findings prove or disprove.

Here are the steps in designing an experiment:

- State the purpose of—and underlying question behind—the experiment you propose to do.
- Recognize the variables involved, and select one that will help you answer the question at hand.
- State a testable hypothesis, an educated guess, about the answer to your question.
- Decide how to change the variable you selected.
- Decide how to measure your results.

Recording Data and Summarizing the Results

Your data should include charts, such as the one you did for these experiments. They should be clearly labeled and easy to read. You may also want to include photos, graphs, or drawings of your experimental setup and results.

If you are preparing an exhibit, you may want to display your results, such as rusted metals or bleached fabrics clearly labeled as to what you did with them. These materials will make your exhibit more interesting for viewers. If you have done a nonexperimental project, explain clearly what your research question was and illustrate your findings.

Related Projects

You can design projects that are similar to these experiments, involving trials and charts of data to summarize results. You could also prepare a model that demonstrates the point that interest you with regard to oxidation-reduction and its effects in everyday life. Or you could do a research project investigating how oxidation-reduction is involved in acid rain or other environmental problems. You could explore the history of scientists who have studied oxidation-reduction and the kinds of experiments that led them to discoveries. The possibilities are numerous.

For More Information

Burns, George, and Nancy Woodman. *Exploring the World of Chemistry.* Danbury, CT: Franklin Watts, 1995. ❖ Outlines several experiments in oxidation.

Fitzgerald, Karen. *The Story of Oxygen.* Danbury, CT: Franklin Watts, 1996. ❖ Explores the history, chemistry, and uses of oxygen.

Gutnik, Martin. *Experiments that Explore Acid Rain.* Millbrook Press, 1992. ❖ Investigates how oxidation reactions affect acid rain, among other experiments.

Mebane, Robert, Thomas Rybolt, and Ronald Perkins. *Adventures with Molecules: Chemistry Experiments for Young People.* Enslow Publishers, 1987. ❖ Outlines more ways to explore oxidation-reduction reactions.

experiment
CENTRAL

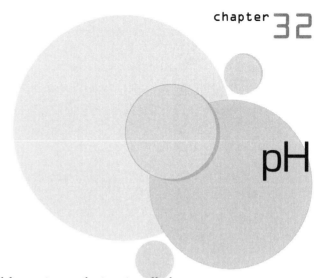

pH

The numerical measurement of **acids** and **bases** in a solution is called **pH** (the abbreviation for potential hydrogen). Acids and bases are groups of chemicals. When dissolved in water, all acids release hydrogen atoms with a positive electric charge (H+). These atoms are known as hydrogen **ions**. The term pH means the strength of the hydrogen ions. The p is derived from the Danish word *potenz* meaning strength; H is the symbol for hydrogen. When dissolved in water, bases produce negatively charged hydroxide ions (OH–). When mixed together in the right proportions, acids and bases **neutralize** each other and form a water and a salt.

In 1909, Danish scientist Soren Peter Lauritz Sorensen, whose wife Margarethe Hoyrup Sorensen assisted him in much of his work, developed the concept of pH for determining hydrogen ion concentration.

Scaling it down

The pH scale ranges from 0 to 14. Very acidic substances are at the lower end of the scale, with 0.0 being the most acidic, and very basic substances are at the upper end of the scale, with 14.0 being the most basic. A pH of 7.0 indicates a substance that is neutral—neither acidic nor basic.

They're everywhere

Acids and bases are present in our daily lives more than we realize. We could not digest food without the diluted hydrochloric acid in our stomachs. Eight special amino acids in the protein foods we eat are

Words to Know

Acid:
A substance that when dissolved in water is capable of reacting with a base to form salts and release hydrogen ions.

Acid rain:
A form of precipitation that is significantly more acidic than neutral water, often as the result of industrial processes and pollution.

Base:
A substance that when dissolved in water is capable of reacting with an acid to form salts and release hydrogen ions.

Dipping universal indicator paper into a solution will indicate if the solution is an acid or a base. (Photo Researchers Inc. Reproduced by permission.)

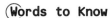

Words to Know

Hypothesis:
An idea in the form of a statement that can be tested by observation and/or experiment.

Indicator:
Pigments that change color when they come into contact with acidic or basic solutions.

Ion:
An atom or group of atoms that carry an electrical charge—either positive or negative—as a result of losing or gaining one or more electrons.

Neutralization:
A chemical reaction in which the mixing of an acidic solution with a basic (alkaline) solution results in a solution that has the properties of neither an acid nor a base.

pH:
(The abbreviation for potential hydrogen.) A measure of acidity or alkalinity of a solution referring to the concentration of hydrogen ions present in a liter of a given fluid.

necessary for good health. Acetic acid is found in vinegar. Sulfuric acid is used in dyes, drugs, explosives, car batteries, and fertilizer. Among the most commonly known bases are ammonia and sodium hydroxide, which is used to make soap.

Are you blue? No, I'm acid

Measuring pH is important to chemists, biologists, bacteriologists, and agriculture experts as well as others in science, medicine, and industry. Your life depends on the right pH of your body fluids, including your blood and digestive juices. Determining soil pH can help a farmer grow better crops because some plants thrive in acidic soils, while others grow better in alkaline (basic) soils. Lime is spread on fields to neutralize soil that is too acidic. The hydrangea plant actually communicates the type of soil it grows in by the color of its flowers. If the soil is alkaline, this plant blooms red. If the soil is acid, it blooms blue.

Quick! Get the litmus paper

But what if you are not a hydrangea plant? How do you determine the pH of a solution? By using an **indicator.** Indicators are pigments that change color when they come into contact with acidic or basic solutions. Litmus paper is an indicator. By dipping litmus paper into liquids and watching the change in color, chemists can tell whether a liquid is an acid or a base.

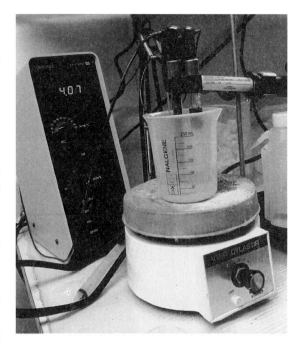

A digital pH meter measures pH. (Photo Researchers Inc. Reproduced by permission.)

Words to Know

Titration:
A procedure in which an acid and a base are slowly mixed to achieve a neutral substance.

Variable:
Something that can affect the results of an experiment.

To determine the pH of a solution, scientists also use a machine called a digital pH meter, which has an electric probe connected to it. The probe is dipped into a solution and measures its pH. A large dial on the meter shows the pH reading. To calculate the total amount of acid or base in a solution, the chemist uses a process called **titration.** Titration is a method of analyzing the makeup of a solution by adding known amounts of a standard solution until a reaction occurs, such as a color change.

It all falls down

Remember the lime the farmer spread on the acidic field? Sometimes lime is added to a lake or stream that has become too acidic because of acid rain. **Acid rain,** an environmental problem that became much worse beginning in the 1950s, is rain, snow, or sleet made unnaturally acidic by sulfur dioxide and nitrogen oxide emissions. The emissions, which mix with air masses, come from the smokestacks of electric power plants that burn coal or from companies that burn high sulfur oil for fuel. Rainfall with a pH of 4, which occurs in the worst acid rain areas, is about one-tenth as acidic as vinegar. Acid rain damages trees and crops and even corrodes stone buildings and statues. Fish are

not able to reproduce when their habitat becomes too acidic. Some larger aquatic plants cannot tolerate the acid and die.

Strong acids can damage metals and human skin. Some weaker acids are used as drugs, including aspirin. Strong bases, such as lye, can blind a person. Baking soda, which is used in baking, toothpaste, and as a cleaner, is a weak base. Measuring a substance's pH can give you valuable information about its structure and makeup.

Experiment 1
Kitchen Chemistry: What is the pH of household chemicals?

Purpose/Hypothesis
The pH scale is used by chemists to determine the ratio of acids to bases present in a solution. The scale ranges from 0 to 14 and indicates whether the solution is more acidic or more basic.

In this experiment you will use an universal indicator to determine the pH of several common household chemicals, including vinegar, baking soda, lemon juice, water, and ammonia. Universal indicators, which change color in the presence of acids and bases over a broad range of the pH scale, exist in nature and are found in a few plants. Red cabbage, grape juice, radish skin, and violet flowers all contain a pigment or coloring that changes in the presence of different chemicals.

The red cabbage "juice" used in this experiment is extracted during the boiling process. This solution is chemically neutral (pH 7), but when added to another substance, the color changes to indicate whether the substance contains a high concentration of an acid or a base. If the substance is an acid, the red cabbage solution will turn pink. If the substance is neutral, the solution will remain purple. If the substance is basic, the solution will become blue, green, or yellow. Yellow indicates a strong base, which may burn your skin on contact.

Before you begin, make an educated guess about the outcome of this experiment based on your knowledge of pH. This educated guess, or prediction, is your **hypothesis.** A hypothesis should explain these things:

- the topic of the experiment
- the variable you will change

The pH scale ranges from 0 to 14 and indicates whether the solution is more acidic or more basic (alkaline).

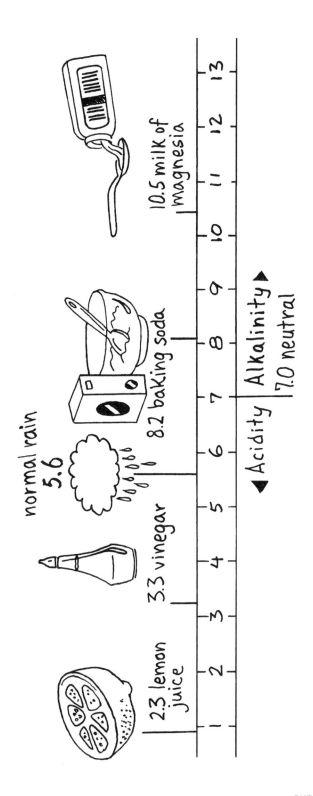

10.5 milk of magnesia

8.2 baking soda

normal rain 5.6

3.3 vinegar

2.3 lemon juice

13 12 11 10 9 8 7 6 5 4 3 2 1

◀ Acidity | Alkalinity ▶
7.0 neutral

 ## What Are the Variables?

Variables are anything that might affect the results of an experiment. Here are the main variables in this experiment:

- the substance being tested
- the age or freshness of the substance
- the concentration of the acidic or basic components of the substance
- the presence and amount of any contaminants in the substance
- the age or freshness of the pH indicator
- the experimenter's ability to distinguish colors

In other words, the variables in this experiment are everything that might affect the pH of the substance and the resulting color of the indicator solution. If you change more than one variable, you will not be able to tell which variable had the most effect on the pH or color.

- the variable you will measure
- what you expect to happen

A hypothesis should be brief, specific, and measurable. It must be something you can test through observation. Your experiment will prove or disprove whether your hypothesis is correct. Here is one possible hypothesis for this experiment: "Vinegar and lemon juice are acids, baking soda and ammonia are bases, and water is neutral."

In this case, the **variable** you will change is the substance being tested, and the variable you will measure is the color of the indicator solution. You expect the indicator solution to show that vinegar and lemon juice are acids, baking soda and ammonia are bases, and water is neutral.

Level of Difficulty

Difficult, because of the care required in using a heat source and in handling ammonia and other chemicals.

experiment
CENTRAL

Materials for Experiment 1.

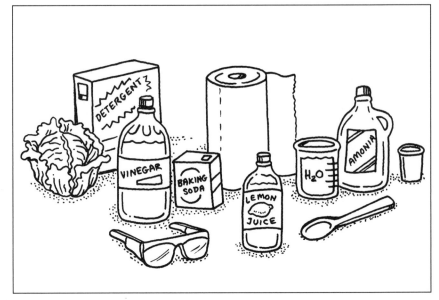

Materials Needed

- red cabbage indicator solution (boil 6 to 8 cabbage leaves in 1 cup of water for 5 minutes, retain only the colored solution and allow to cool)
- household chemicals: vinegar, baking soda, lemon juice, water, ammonia, white or clear detergent, etc.
- cups (3.5-ounce clear plastic) or test tubes (glass or plastic)
- measuring spoons
- goggles
- paper towels (for cleanup)

Approximate Budget

$2 for the red cabbage, which is necessary for this experiment.

Timetable

1 hour.

Step-by-Step Instructions

1. Place a small amount (approximately 1/2 teaspoon) of one chemical into the cup. Wash the measuring spoon.

2. Place an equal amount of indicator solution (red cabbage water) in the same cup. Again, wash the measuring spoon.

3. Record the resulting color change of the indicator solution.

experiment
CENTRAL

How to Experiment Safely

Adult supervision is necessary for this experiment. Treat each chemical as if it were dangerous, and do not inhale the odors, especially from the ammonia. Do not eat or drink while conducting this experiment. Wear goggles to prevent eye injury. Wash your hands immediately if they come in contact with any of the chemicals. Consult your science teacher before you substitute any chemicals for the ones listed in this experiment.

4. Determine the chemical property of the substance—acid, base, or neutral.

5. In clean cups, repeat this procedure for each of the other chemicals.

Summary of Results

Record your results in a journal or notebook. Go back to your hypothesis and determine whether your original guesses were correct. Write a paragraph summarizing your findings.

Here is a general rule of thumb for acids and bases:

- Acids are corrosive but lose their acidity when combined with bases.
- Bases feel slippery when they come in contact with the skin; they lose their alkalinity when mixed with acids. (But do not test bases by touching them; they can burn your skin.)
- Salts are formed when acids and bases react.

Troubleshooter's Guide

Be aware of contamination. Always make sure the utensils and cups are clean. Use only fresh chemicals that have not spoiled. If you are not getting the desired results, place a scoop of baking soda (sodium bicarbonate) into a cup that has been washed, rinsed, and dried. Make sure you use a clean spoon. Pour in some indicator solution and stir. The resulting color should be blue, indicating a base.

Change the Variables

You can vary this experiment in several ways. Try comparing different brand-name items or testing items that have spoiled. For instance, milk when fresh is base but when spoiled is an acid.

Experiment 2

Chemical Titration: What is required to change a substance from an acid or a base into a neutral solution?

Purpose/Hypothesis

After you understand how to use indicators, you can begin testing and manipulating chemicals. Here is a general description of how acids and bases mix and the results. Acids produce a H+ particle called a hydrogen ion. Bases produce an OH– particle called a hydroxide ion. These H+ and OH– ions can join to form H2O or water, a neutral substance. The leftover substance is a salt.

The chemical formula for a typical acid-base reaction between hydrochloric acid and sodium hydroxide is illustrated. The resulting products of this reaction are neutral sodium chloride (salt) and water.

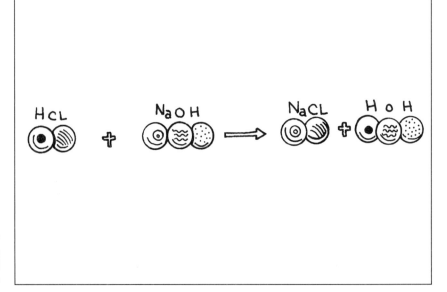

The chemical formula for a typical acid-base reaction between hydrochloric acid and sodium hydroxide.

What Are the Variables?

Variables are anything that might affect the results of an experiment. Here are the variables for this experiment:

- the acid or base being tested
- the age or freshness of the acid and base
- the concentration of the acidic or basic components (many acids are diluted in water)
- the presence and amount of any contaminants in the acid and base
- the amount of acid added to the base, and vice versa
- the age or freshness of the pH indicator
- the experimenter's ability to distinguish colors

In other words, the variables in this experiment are everything that might affect the pH of the substance and the resulting color of the indicator solution. If you change more than one variable, you will not be able to tell which variable had the most effect on the pH or color.

When an acid and a base combine to form a neutral solution, the procedure is called a titration reaction.

Before you begin, make an educated guess about the outcome of this experiment based on your knowledge of pH. This educated guess, or prediction, is your **hypothesis.** A hypothesis should explain these things:

- the topic of the experiment
- the variable you will change
- the variable you will measure
- what you expect to happen

A hypothesis should be brief, specific, and measurable. It must be something you can test through observation. Your experiment will prove or disprove whether your hypothesis is correct. Here is one possible hypothesis for this experiment: "A basic substance can be neutralized by the addition of an acid, and vice versa."

In this case, the **variable** you will change is the amount of acid being added to the base (or base to acid), and the variable you will measure is the color of the indicator solution. You expect the indicator solution to show a color indicating the basic pH changes to a neutral pH with the addition of an acid, and vice versa.

Level of Difficulty

Difficult, because of the care required in using a heat source and in handling chemicals.

Materials Needed

- red cabbage indicator solution (refer to Experiment 1 for instructions)
- vinegar
- baking soda
- stomach antacids (such as Tums)
- baking powder
- clear plastic cups
- measuring spoons
- goggles

Materials for Experiment 2.

How to Experiment Safely

Adult supervision is necessary for this experiment. Treat each chemical as if it were dangerous. Do not eat or drink while conducting this experiment. Wear goggles to prevent eye injury. Wash your hands immediately if they come in contact with any of the chemicals. Consult your science teacher before you substitute any chemicals for the ones listed in this experiment.

When acids and bases react to form a salt, the reaction can be violent. Gases, flames, heat, and other forms of energy can be released. In other words, use caution!

Approximate Budget

$2 to $10.

Timetable

1 hour.

Step-by-Step Instructions

1. In a cup place 1 teaspoon of baking soda.

2. In the same cup place an equal amount of indicator solution, and then stir.

3. Note the color of the solution.

4. In the same cup slowly pour some vinegar. Watch the violent acid-base reaction, and stop when the solution turns purple.

Step 4: Slowly pour vinegar into the cup and watch the violent acid-base reaction.

5. If you add too much vinegar, the solution may turn pink. Slowly sprinkle more baking soda into the cup until the purple color reappears.

Summary of Results

When the baking soda (a base) was added to the indicator, the color changed from purple to blue indicating the presence of OH– ions (a base) with a pH of greater than 7. When the vinegar (an acid) was added, the H+ ions reacted with the OH– ions and produced water (a purple neutral solution, with a pH of 7). The gas CO_2 was produced during the reaction. When an acid and a base are joined equally, the resulting solution is neutral. You have caused a titration reaction. Summarize the results of your experiment in writing.

Change the Variables

You can vary this experiment in several ways. Try adding substances such as antacids to vinegar and indicator solutions. Test the pH of baking powder, which is an acid and a base in a powdered mixture.

 Design Your Own Experiment

How to Select a Topic Relating to this Concept

Here is your chance to create a fun experiment about a topic that interests you. Chemistry is a great topic to experiment in because it is part of your everyday life. Everything from the detergent that washes your clothes to the vinegar in salad dressing is made up of chemicals, and so are you! Find an area of chemistry that interests you and start to investigate it. Cleaners, cosmetics, medicine, and food are some areas that you may want to examine.

Check the For More Information section and talk with your science teacher or school or community media specialist to start gathering information on pH questions that interest you. As you consider possible experiments, be sure to discuss them with your science teacher or another knowledgeable adult before trying them. Some chemicals can be dangerous.

Steps in the Scientific Method

To do an original experiment, you need to plan carefully and think things through. Otherwise, you might not be sure of what question you are answering, what you are or should be measuring, or what your findings may prove or disprove.

Here are the steps in designing an experiment:

- State the purpose of—and the underlying question behind—the experiment you propose to do.
- Recognize the variables involved, and select one that will help you answer the question at hand.
- State a testable hypothesis, an educated guess about the answer to your question.
- Decide how to change the variable you selected.
- Decide how to measure your results.

Recording Data and Summarizing the Results
Keep a journal and record your notes and measurements in it. Your experiment can then be utilized by others to answer their questions about your topic.

Related Projects
After you have chosen a topic to examine, develop an experiment to go with it. For example, you might want to investigate the power of detergents or cleaners. Since grass stains on jeans are common, your experiment could be to determine what detergent works best to remove them.

For More Information
Adams, Richard, and Robert Gardner. *Ideas for Science Projects.* New York: Franklin Watts, 1996. ❖ Well-organized science projects for middle-grade students.

Newmark, Ann. *Eyewitness Science: Chemistry.* London: Dorling Kindersley, 1993. ❖ Great visual examples and interesting facts that include pH.

chapter 33

Photosynthesis

To get our food, we go to the supermarket, pick vegetables or fruit from our gardens, or cast a rod in our favorite fishing hole. A plant, however, makes its own food using sunlight as its major energy source in a process called **photosynthesis.** In fact, the term **photosynthesis** means "putting together by light."

Shining the light on vegetables

In the eighteenth century, Jan Ingenhousz, a Dutch physician and plant **physiologist,** proved that sunlight was essential to the life activities of green plants. In 1779, he published experiments showing that plants have two respiratory cycles. At night, plants absorb oxygen and exhale carbon dioxide, just as animals do, but during the day the cycle is reversed. Another eighteenth-century scientist, Englishman Joseph Priestley, made similar discoveries about plant **respiration;** but it was Ingenhousz who proved through his vegetable experiments that it was *only* in the presence of light that plants absorbed carbon dioxide and gave off oxygen. This was a major discovery because until then most people thought the soil was the only source of a plant's nutrients.

How it works

Think of a plant's leaf as a solar panel. Just like the flat glass panels you see on rooftops, a leaf's flat surface makes it an efficient sunlight absorber. Within each leaf cell are up to a hundred disc-shaped **chloroplasts.** Chloroplasts have a green **pigment** called **chlorophyll,** which traps light.

Words to Know

Carotene
Yellow-orange pigment in plants.

Chlorophyll:
A green pigment found in plants that absorbs sunlight, providing the energy used in photosynthesis for the conversion of carbon dioxide and water to complex carbohydrates.

Chloroplasts:
Small structures in plant cells that contain chlorophyll and in which the process of photosynthesis takes place.

experiment
CENTRAL

We know that sunlight is actually a spectrum of many colors that have different wavelengths. The pigments in plants absorb different wavelengths of the sunlight spectrum. Chlorophyll is not the only pigment in plants, but it is the most plentiful pigment. It reflects the green part of the spectrum, which makes plants look green to the human eye, but absorbs other parts of the spectrum. Other pigments, such as **carotene** and **xanthophyll** reflect yellow-orange and yellow spectrum colors. These pigments act as a support team to chlorophyll.

Sunlight supplies the energy. Chlorophyll turns the switch that powers a plant's chemical reactions. Those reactions include taking carbon dioxide from the atmosphere, plus water and inorganic chemicals from the soil, and converting them into oxygen and **glucose.** Glucose is needed in every part of the plant. Cellulose, the tough, fibrous part of the plant, is formed from glucose. Starch, another glucose by-product, is stored within the roots, leaves, or stems of plants. Pores on the underside of the leaf let gases in and out. Tubes called **xylem** carry water throughout the plant; tubes called **phloem** distribute the food.

Light intensity, temperature, and water supply are some of the key factors that affect the rate of photosynthesis. In rain forests, plants grow in abundance,because the weather there is rainy and warm, and the Sun's rays are more intense.

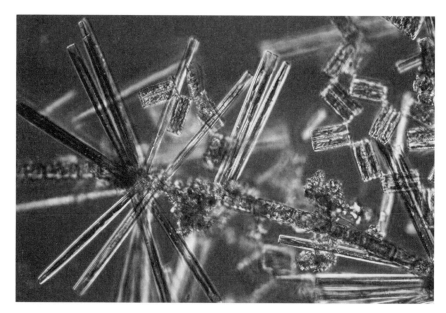

Phytoplankton are underwater plants that utilize photosynthesis to produce oxygen. (Peter Arnold Inc. Reproduced by permission.)

Need oxygen? Get a plant

The carbon dioxide given off by animals is consumed by plants. Plants on land and in the sea replace the oxygen taken in by animals. That is why there is so much concern for preserving forests, green spaces, and oceans. Besides being animal habitats, they are oxygen producers. Without plants, we would all die.

Interestingly, most of Earth's photosynthesis does not take place on land. Over 75 percent of photosynthesis processes on Earth actually takes place in our oceans. Chlorophyll is the vital link in photosynthesis in marine plants as well. But these underwater organisms have larger concentrations of other pigments than their plant "cousins" on land. Because little light penetrates below a depth of 330 feet (100 meters), photosynthesis takes place in the upper part of the ocean called the **euphotic zone.** Plants that live in this zone are called **phytoplankton.**

During photosynthesis, plants consume carbon dioxide produced by animals and replace oxygen consumed by animals. Unlocking the keys of this balanced activity through experiments will help you appreciate the hidden benefits of our national parks, nature preserves, and oceans. Plants are not green things that just sit there, but vital, living organisms that help us stay healthy.

Words to Know

Euphotic zone:
The upper part of the ocean where sunlight penetrates, supporting plant life, such as phytoplankton.

Glucose:
A simple sugar broken down in cells to produce energy.

Hypothesis:
An idea phrased in the form of a statement that can be tested by observation and/or experiment.

Phloem:
Plant tissue consisting of elongated cells that transport carbohydrates and other nutrients.

Photosynthesis:
Chemical process by which plants containing chlorophyll use sunlight to manufacture their own food by converting carbon dioxide and water to carbohydrates, releasing oxygen as a by-product.

Experiment 1
Photosynthesis: How does light affect plant growth?

Purpose/Hypothesis

This experiment deals with the concept of photosynthesis and how different wavelengths of light affect plant growth. Plants contain different pigments, including chlorophyll, carotene, and xanthophyll, so they can respond to different wavelengths. In this experiment, three different colors of light will be used to grow plants. The three colors will represent different wavelengths of light: red—long; yellow—medium; and violet or blue—short. A fourth plant will be grown under a white light, which contains all wavelengths. The amount of growth for each plant will demonstrate which color light promotes the most plant growth.

To begin your experiment, use what you know about photosynthesis to make an educated guess about light color and plant growth. This educated guess, or prediction, is your **hypothesis**. A hypothesis should explain these things:

What Are the Variables?

Variables are anything that might affect the results of the experiment. Here are the main variables in this experiment:

- the types of plants chosen
- the color of light
- the intensity of light
- the amount of water provided to each plant
- the type of soil
- the surrounding air temperature

In other words, the variables in this experiment are everything that might affect the growth of the plants. If you change more than one variable, you will not be able to tell which variable had the most effect on plant growth.

Words to Know

Physiologist:
A scientist who studies the functions and processes of living organisms.

Phytoplankton:
Microscopic aquatic plants that live suspended in the water.

Pigment:
A substance that displays a color because of the wavelengths of light it reflects.

Respiration:
The physical process that supplies oxygen to an animal's body. It also describes a series of chemical reactions that take place inside cells. In plants, at night or in the dark, the process is the same as in animals. In light, plants absorb carbon dioxide to use in photosynthesis, and give off oxygen.

Variable:
Something that can affect the results of an experiment.

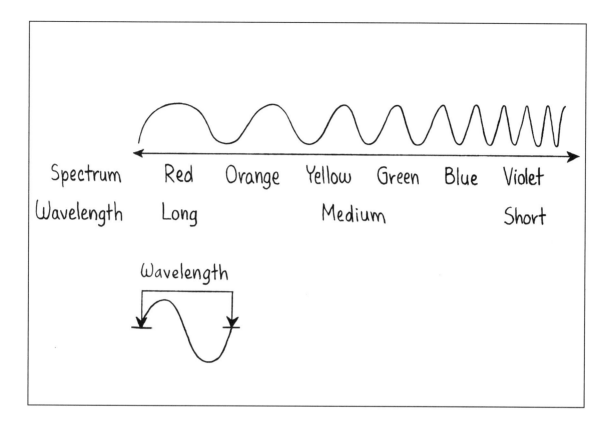

- the topic of the experiment
- the **variable** you will change
- the variable you will measure
- what you expect to happen

A hypothesis should be brief, specific, and measurable. It must be something you can test through observation. Your experiment will prove or disprove whether your hypothesis is correct. Here is one possible hypothesis for this experiment: "Plants grown under white light will grow the most because white light contains all the wavelengths that plants can use in photosynthesis and most closely duplicates natural sunlight."

In this case, the variable you will change is the color, or wavelength, of light, and the variable you will measure is the amount of plant growth over a period of several weeks. If the plants under the white light grow more than those under the colored lights, you will know your hypothesis is correct.

Words to Know

Xanthophyll:
Yellow pigment in plants.

Xylem:
Plant tissue of elongated, thick-walled cells that transport water and mineral nutrients.

Materials for Experiment 1.

Level of Difficulty

Moderate, since the plants in this experiment may require daily attention for a few weeks.

Materials Needed

- scissors
- 4 lamps (desk lamps with reflectors are best)
- 4 cardboard boxes, 18 inches (46 centimeters) square
- 4 light bulbs (25-watt), in white, red, yellow, and violet or blue
- 4 pots filled with soil
- 40-80 bean or corn seeds (These seeds sprout and grow rapidly, so results can be seen in two weeks. Use the same type of seeds in all pots.)

Approximate Budget

$3 for each light bulb and $3 for bean and corn seeds.

Timetable

Approximately 4 weeks, during which 15 minutes of daily attention is required, plus 1 hour to set things up.

Step-By-Step Instructions

1. Plant 10 to 20 seedlings in each pot. Water generously and allow the water to drain.

How to Experiment Safely

Use caution when handling hot lamps. Be sure the lamps and light bulbs are not touching the boxes or plants. Turn off the lights and move the lamps aside before watering the plants to avoid a possible electrical shock.

2. Cut a hole into the top of your boxes. The hole should be 2 inches (5 centimeters) smaller in diameter than the diameter of the lamp. Try to place the hole in the center of the box top. Cut a door in the side of each box so that the door can be closed during the day to block outside light.

3. Locate the boxes side-by-side on a table away from windows in a warm, but not hot, room. Place a lamp with a different color light bulb over each box. Label each box as illustrated.

4. Place a plant inside each box under the light.

5. Plug in the lamps and turn them on.

6. After the seeds sprout, open each door every day and record the height of each plant on your results chart.

Steps 3 and 4: Place a lamp with a different color light bulb over each box. Label each box as illustrated. Place a plant inside each box under the light.

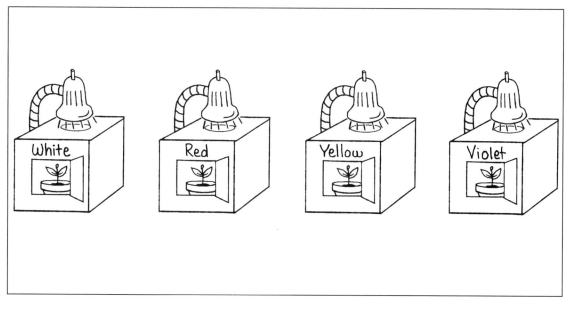

7. Leave the lights on each day for approximately 8 to 12 hours. Turn them on in the morning, and shut them off at night. Remember to keep the doors in the boxes closed.

8. Sprinkle water over the soil every other day. Never allow the soil to completely dry out. Remember to turn the lights off and move the lamps aside before watering the plants to avoid a possible electrical shock. Replace the lamps when you are finished.

9. After 2 to 4 weeks, study your charted results and summarize them.

Summary of Results

After the experiment is finished, collect the final data and organize it into usable statistics and charts. Graph the plant heights for a visual comparison of plant growth. Determine which wavelength/color affects growth the most. Reflect on your hypothesis. Which color/wavelength of light was most beneficial for plant growth?

Change the Variables

Different plant species contain varying amounts of pigments. Instead of varying the color of light, you could vary the plant being tested—either by growing different seeds or by using different small house plants.

You could also test the effect of varying the intensity of light, which is what you can do in Experiment #2.

Troubleshooter's Guide

Here is a problem you may encounter, some possible causes, and ways to fix the problem.

Problem: All the plants are starting to wilt, turn yellow, or fall over.

Possible cause: The plants may be in shock from being removed from their normal environment. Grow the plants outside the box, indoors, for one week before starting the experiment again.

Possible cause: The lamps are too close to the plants, causing them to wilt from the heat. Raise the lamp a few inches and try again.

Experiment 2
Light Intensity: How does the intensity of light affect plant growth?

Purpose/Hypothesis

This experiment deals with the amount of light required for photosynthesis and growth. In this experiment, three wattages of light bulbs—40 watt, 25 watt, and 5 watt—will be used to determine how the different amounts of light intensity affect plant growth. A fourth plant will have no light bulb. In general, the more light present, the better a plant responds in its growth and vigor. However, light can also scorch or burn a plant if it is too intense.

To begin the experiment, use what you know about photosynthesis to make an educated guess about how light intensity will affect plant growth. This educated guess, or prediction, is your **hypothesis**. A hypothesis should explain these things:

What Are the Variables?

Variables are anything that might affect the results of an experiment. Here are the main variables in this experiment:

- the types of plants chosen
- the intensity of light
- the amount of water provided to each plant
- the type of soil
- the surrounding air temperature

In other words, the variables in this experiment are everything that might affect the growth of the plants. If you change more than one variable, you will not be able to tell which variable had the most effect on plant growth.

Plants can be categorized into those having a low, medium, or high preference for light. For this experiment, an ivy was chosen because it has a medium light preference.

- the topic of the experiment
- the **variable** you will change
- the variable you will measure
- what you expect to happen

A hypothesis should be brief, specific, and measurable. It must be something you can test through observation. Your experiment will prove or disprove whether your hypothesis is correct. Here is one possible hypothesis for this experiment: "A 25-watt light bulb will promote the most plant growth because its intensity is neither too dim nor too bright."

In this case, the variable you will change is the intensity of the light, and the variable you will measure is the amount of plant growth over a period of several weeks. If the plant under the 25-watt light bulb grows the most, you will know your hypothesis is correct.

Level of Difficulty
Moderate because of the duration of the experiment. (It takes approximately 4 weeks to cause a noticeable result.)

Materials Needed
- scissors
- 3 lamps (desk lamps with reflectors are best)
- 4 cardboard boxes, 18 inches (46 centimeters) square
- 3 light bulbs: one 40-watt, one 25-watt, one 5-watt
- 4 potted ivy plants

Approximate Budget
$20 for light bulbs and plants.

Timetable
4 weeks, including 5 minutes a day for watering and recording growth, plus 1 hour for set up.

Step-By-Step Instructions
1. Cut a hole into the top of three boxes. The hole should be 2 inches (5 centimeters) smaller in diameter than the diameter of the lamp. Try to place the hole in the center of the box top. Do not cut a hole in the top of the fourth box.

2. Cut a door into each box, following the diagram illustrated.

experiment
CENTRAL

3. Place a lamp with a light bulb over each box with a hole in it. Label each box.

4. Place a potted plant inside each of the four boxes.

5. Record the health of each plant. Measure its approximate size.

6. Plug in lamps and turn them on.

7. Keep the lights on for 8 to 12 hours daily. Keep the doors closed to block outside light.

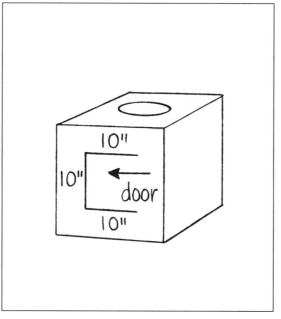

Step 2: Cut a door into each box. Door should be 10 inches wide on all sides; only three sides are cut with the fourth side acting as a hinge.

Steps 3 and 4: Place a lamp with a light bulb over each box with a hole in it and label each box. Place a potted plant inside each of the four boxes.

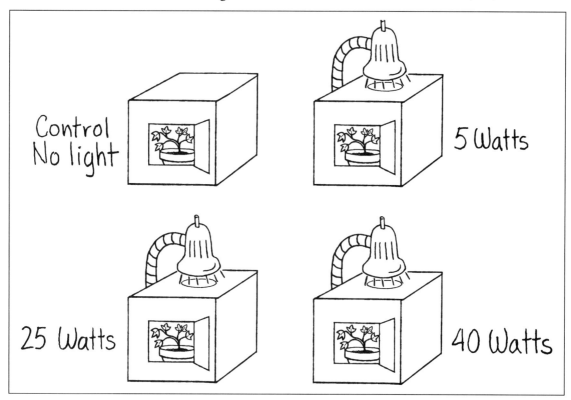

Control No light

5 Watts

25 Watts

40 Watts

How to Experiment Safely

Use caution when handling hot lamps. Be sure the lamps and light bulbs are not touching the boxes or plants. Do not use bulbs with an intensity greater than 40 watts to avoid the possibility of fire. Turn off the lights and move the lamps aside before watering the plants to avoid a possible electrical shock.

8. Water the plants every other day. Remember to turn off the lights and move the lamps aside before watering the plants to avoid a possible electrical shock.

Step 9: Each week record the changes in each plant. Illustration shows the likely outcome after four weeks.

9. Check on the plants daily. Record any changes in health, such as loss of leaves, plants turning brown, or plants growing toward light.

No light	5 Watts	25 Watts	40 Watts
Dead	No leaves Green stem	Old leaves died New leaves are smaller	Large, healthy plant Lots of dark-green leaves

Troubleshooter's Guide

Here is a problem you may encounter, a possible cause, and a way to solve the problem.

Problem: All the plants lost their leaves.

Possible cause: The plants are in shock. Grow them outside the box inside the house for a week or two before starting the experiment.

Mark the headings Week 1, 2, 3, and 4, and record the changes in each plant.

10. After 4 weeks, the plant with no light will probably be dead and the experiment will be concluded.

Summary of Results

After the experiment is completed, collect your data and display it for others to view. Make drawings of plants to demonstrate the effects of light intensity. Reflect on your hypothesis and draw some conclusions. What was the best wattage or light intensity for the plants? If your hypothesis was that the 25-watt light would be best, and it turned out that the 40-watt light was actually the best, you weren't wrong—you just got a different result than predicted. You still learned something from the experiment.

Change the Variables

Just as in Experiment #1, one way to change the variables is to change the plants being tested. Go to a plant nursery and find a type of plant that likes a low intensity light. Repeat the experiment to see which wattage bulb produces the best growth with the new plant.

 # Design Your Own Experiment

How to Select a Topic Relating to this Concept

Photosynthesis is essential for a plant's survival and growth. Air, water, light, nutrients, and temperature are crucial elements that play a part in photosynthesis. You can select from the elements needed for photosynthesis to conduct an experiment. For example: temperature affects the function of the pigments responsible for photosynthesis. You can experiment to determine at what temperature photosynthesis stops in trees, that is, when they go into dormancy.

Check the For More Information section and talk with your science teacher or school or community media specialist to start gathering information on photosynthesis questions that interest you. As you consider possible experiments, be sure to discuss them with your science teacher or another knowledgeable adult before trying them. Some of them might be dangerous.

Steps in the Scientific Method

Here is your chance to answer questions or discover new facts. Design an experiment about a topic that interests you. To do this, you must follow some guidelines to help you stick to your goal and get useful information.

Here are the steps in designing an experiment:

- State the purpose of—and the underlying question behind—the experiment you propose to do.
- Recognize the variable involved, and select one that will help you answer the question at hand.
- State a testable hypothesis, an educated guess about the answer to your question.
- Decide how to change the variable you selected.
- Decide how to measure your results.

Recording Data and Summarizing the Results

Experimenting is a means by which we discover the answers to our questions. It is important to record all the changes in the experiment as well as conclusions drawn from it. Others may use your experiment to answer questions or solve related problems regarding your topic.

Related Projects

If you decide to test temperature and its effects, you may want to choose a plant that drops its leaves, known as deciduous, and monitor the temperature outside. In this sample experiment, all you have to do is choose a plant species, such as white oak, and monitor the average temperature when it drops its leaves.

For More Information

Bonnet, Robert L., and G. Daniel Keen. *Botany: 49 Science Fair Projects.* Blue Ridge Summit, PA: Tab Books, 1989. ❖ Features seven projects on photosynthesis in Chapter 3.

Lammert, John M. *Plants: How to Do A Successful Project.* Vero Beach, FL: Rourke Publications, Inc., 1992. ❖ Includes a chapter on photosynthesis.

chapter 34

Potential and Kinetic Energy

Energy is involved in nearly everything we do. It is defined as the ability to do work, to set an object in motion. There are several different kinds of energy. **Kinetic energy** is the energy an object has when it is in motion. Vibration, forward motion, turning, and spinning are all examples of kinetic energy. Kinetic energy is directly proportional to the **mass** of an object. If two objects move at the same speed, and one has twice the mass of the other, the object with twice the mass will have twice the kinetic energy.

Potential energy is the energy an object has because of its position; it is energy waiting to be released. For example, a weight suspended above the ground has potential energy because it can be set in motion by gravity. Compressed or extended springs also have potential energy.

Thermal energy is the kinetic energy of atoms vibrating within matter. The faster the atoms move, the hotter the object becomes. **Electrical energy** is the kinetic energy resulting from the motion of electrons within any object that conducts electricity. **Chemical energy** is the potential energy stored in molecules. Thermal, electrical, and chemical energy are all forms of kinetic or potential energy.

What laws control energy?

One of the most fundamental laws of physics is that energy cannot be created or destroyed, only transformed from one form into another. For example, if a suspended weight falls, its potential energy becomes kinetic energy. When a car burns fuel, the fuel's chemical energy is transformed into thermal energy, which in turn, is transformed into kinetic energy by the engine to make the car move.

Words to Know

Chemical energy:
Potential energy stored in molecules.

Control experiment:
A set-up that is identical to the experiment but is not affected by the variable that affects the experimental group. Results from the control experiment are compared to results from the actual experiment.

Electrical energy:
Kinetic energy resulting from the motion of electrons within any object that conducts electricity.

As one ball hits another, it transfers some of its kinetic energy to that ball. (Photo Researchers Inc. Reproduced by permission.)

Energy can also be transferred from one object to another. Think about a game of pool. When a moving ball hits a still one, the moving ball stops and the still one begins to move. The majority of the first ball's kinetic energy has been transferred to the second ball, while a small amount has been converted to thermal energy by the collision. If you could measure the temperature on the surface of each ball, you would find there was a slight rise in temperature at the point of contact. The total amount of energy involved—kinetic and thermal—remains the same. No energy was created or destroyed by the collision.

Who wrote these laws?

The person who laid the groundwork for the study of energy was English mathematician and physicist Isaac Newton (1642–1727). Newton developed the laws of motion, which describe how objects are acted upon by forces. Newton's ideas formed the basis for much of physics, in fact. He studied at Cambridge University, where he excelled in mathematics and developed the field of calculus while he was still a student. Newton later became a professor at Cambridge, where he built the first reflecting telescope and studied optics.

He published his most important work in 1687, the *Principia Mathematica*. This book describes Newton's three laws of motion and the law of gravitation, which are a major part of the foundation of modern science. Newton also had an interesting life. He became

Words to Know

Energy:
The ability to cause an action or to perform work.

Hypothesis:
An idea in the form of a statement that can be tested by observations and/or experiment.

Kinetic energy:
The energy of an object or system due to its motion.

Mass:
Measure of the total amount of matter in an object.

Potential energy:
The energy of an object or system due to its position.

OPPOSITE PAGE: The position of the weight above the ground gives it potential energy. (Photo Researchers Inc. Reproduced by permission.)

experiment
CENTRAL

Master of Mint in England, where he supervised the making of money, and later became the first scientist to be knighted.

What questions do you have about energy? In the following experiments, you will have a chance to explore the topics of potential and kinetic energy. You will learn more about how these forms of energy affect us and everything we do.

Experiment 1
Measuring Energy: How does the height of an object affect its potential energy?

Purpose/Hypothesis

In this experiment, you will drop a rubber ball and measure its rebound height. When you pick up the ball and raise it to a certain height, your body is performing work, and the ball is gaining potential energy as a result. When you release the ball, this potential energy changes to kinetic energy as the force of gravity causes the ball to gain speed. When the ball hits the ground, its kinetic energy changes back to potential energy as the ball comes to a stop and is compressed by the impact. A split second later, the potential energy of this compression propels the ball back into the air, giving it kinetic energy again. Finally, as the ball reaches the maximum height of its rebound, its kinetic energy is converted back into potential energy, as measured by its height above the ground.

To begin the experiment, use what you know about potential and kinetic energy to make an educated guess about the relation between the ball's initial drop height and its rebound height. This educated guess, or prediction, is your **hypothesis.** A hypothesis should explain these things:

- the topic of the experiment
- the **variable** you will change
- the variable you will measure
- what you expect to happen

A hypothesis should be brief, specific, and measurable. It must be something you can test through observation. Your experiment will prove or disprove whether your hypothesis is correct. Here is one possible hypothesis for this experiment: "The higher the height from

What Are the Variables?

Variables are anything that might affect the results of an experiment. Here are the main variables in this experiment:

- the mass of the ball
- the material it is made of
- the surface on which it bounces
- the height from which it is dropped
- the force with which it is dropped
- the height to which it bounces back

In other words, the variables in this experiment are everything that might affect the rebound height of the ball. If you change more than one variable, you will not be able to tell which variable had the most effect on the rebound height.

which the ball falls, the greater its potential energy and the higher it will bounce."

In this case, the variable you will change will be the height from which you drop the ball. The variable you will measure will be the height it reaches when it bounces back. If the height of the ball's rebound increases as you increase the drop height, you will know your hypothesis is correct.

Setting up a **control experiment** will help you isolate one variable. Only one variable will change between the control and the experimental bounce, and that is the height from which you drop the ball. For the control, you will drop the ball from 3 feet (about 1 meter) high. For the experiment, you will change the height for each drop.

You will measure the height to which the ball bounces back each time. If the ball dropped from higher distances bounces back to higher heights, your hypothesis is correct.

Level of Difficulty

Easy.

How to Experiment Safely

In selecting your bouncing location, choose a place where you will not knock over or break anything.

Materials Needed

- rubber ball
- flat wood or concrete floor on which to bounce the ball
- paper and pencils
- masking tape
- measuring tape, about 6 feet (2 meters) long

Approximate Budget

$3 for a rubber ball.

Timetable

About 1 hour.

Step-by-Step Instructions

1. With your measuring tape, measure up a wall 3 feet (about 1 meter) from the floor and mark this level with a piece of masking tape. This will be your control height.

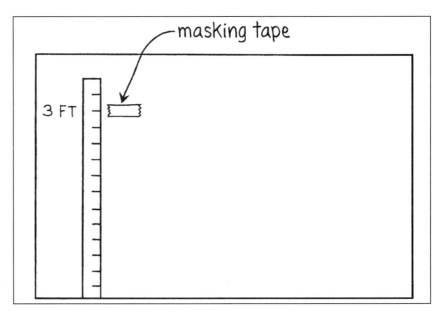

masking tape

Steps 1 and 2: Measure 3 feet up a wall and mark; tape the measuring tape to the wall with the "zero" end at the floor.

3 FT

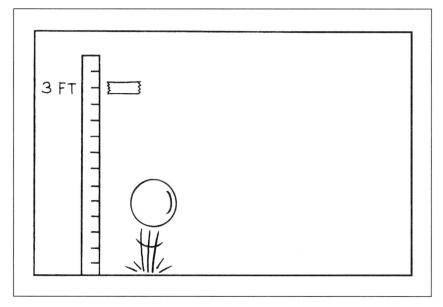

Step 3: Hold the ball slightly away from the wall at the 3-foot height and simply drop it.

2. Tape your measuring tape to the wall with the "zero" end at the floor. You will use it to measure the heights of the bouncing ball.

3. Hold the ball slightly away from the wall at the 3-foot height and simply drop it. Do not use any force, as it will affect your results. Watch closely and use the measuring tape to determine how high the ball bounced. Repeat the drop several times and average the

Recording chart for Experiment 1.

Trial	Height Dropped	Height Bounced
1 (control)	3 feet	
2		
3		
4		
⋮		

bounce heights. Record the height from which you dropped it and the average height to which it bounced.

4. Now drop the same ball several times from at least 12 inches (30 centimeters) higher or lower than the control level. Record its bounce heights, taking an average for each dropping height.

5. Repeat this procedure for at least five different heights, recording each height and averaging each bounce height.

Summary of Results

Study the results on your chart. Did the drop height affect how high the ball bounced back? Was your hypothesis correct? Did the ball rebound as high as the drop height? If not, why not? Be sure to summarize what you discovered.

Troubleshooter's Guide

Below are some problems that may occur during this experiment, possible causes, and ways to remedy the problems.

Problem: It is difficult to accurately measure the bounce height.

Possible cause:

1. You are measuring the bounce against a wall that is too close to the color of the ball. Try bouncing with a ball that is significantly darker or lighter than the wall you are measuring against.

2. Your measuring tape is difficult to read. Try marking off heights with chalk or masking tape so that they are easier to read.

Problem: The ball bounces so high you cannot see where the bounce ends.

Possible cause:

1. The ball you are using is too rubbery. Try using a slightly less bouncy ball.

2. You are exerting force when you drop the ball. Do not push down when you drop the ball. Simply let it fall from your hand.

Change the Variables

You can vary this experiment in several ways. For example, instead of changing the height, change the weight (mass) of the ball. Use a rubber ball that is much heavier and one that is much lighter, all dropped from the same height. (Change only one variable at a time.) Weigh each ball before you drop it. Use the ball from this experiment as your control. Record each bounce height again. What do you find?

You can also try using different kinds of balls, such as tennis balls or golf balls. How are they affected? What do you think makes the difference?

Experiment 2
Using Energy: Build a roller coaster

Purpose/Hypothesis

Potential energy, provided by the force of gravity pulling on an object, is converted into kinetic energy as an object falls from a height. The amount of potential energy an object has is revealed by the speed with which it moves once released.

You can calculate potential energy using the formula PE=mgh, where m is mass, g is the acceleration of gravity 32.2 feet/second^2 (9.8 meters/second^2), and h is the height of the object in feet (meters). You can calculate kinetic energy using the formula KE=(0.5)mv^2, where m is mass, and v is the velocity of the object in feet/second (meters/second). The speed with which the object moves and the height to which it returns also indicate how much potential energy is being converted into kinetic energy and back to potential energy. You can explore this idea by watching a roller coaster.

In this experiment, you will build your own roller coaster and roll a marble on it to demonstrate potential and kinetic energy. Do you have an idea about how a marble will behave on a homemade roller coaster? Where will it move the fastest? Will it have enough energy from rolling down one hill to roll up the next hill?

To begin the experiment, use what you know about potential and kinetic energy to make an educated guess about how the marble will

experiment
CENTRAL

What Are the Variables?

Variables are anything that might affect the results of an experiment. Here are the main variables in this experiment:

- the height of the first hill and the second hill

- the amount of friction between the track and the marble

- the amount of force or "push" you apply to the marble when you release it

    In other words, the variables are anything that might affect the height the marble will reach on the second hill. If you change more than one variable, you will not be able to tell which variable had the most effect on the results.

behave. This educated guess, or prediction, is your **hypothesis**. A hypothesis should explain these things:

- the topic of the experiment
- the **variable** you will change
- the variable you will measure
- what you expect to happen

A hypothesis should be brief, specific, and measurable. It must be something you can test through observation. Your experiment will prove or disprove whether your hypothesis is correct. Here is one possible hypothesis for this experiment: "The higher the first hill of the roller coaster, the higher the marble will climb on the second hill."

In this case, the variable you will change will be the height of the first hill, and the variable you will measure will be the height the marble climbs on the second hill. If the marble climbs higher on the second hill when the height of the first hill is raised, you will know your hypothesis is correct.

Only one variable will change between the control and experimental set-up, and that is the height at which the marble starts to roll. For the control, you will start your marble from a hill at 2 feet (0.6 meters) above ground. For your experiments, you will vary the heights

OPPOSITE PAGE: A roller coaster uses both potential and kinetic energy. (Photo Researchers Inc. Reproduced by permission.)

of the first hill. You will measure the heights that the marble climbs on the second hill to compare the amount of kinetic energy produced by the potential energy of the initial drop.

Level of Difficulty
Moderate.

Materials Needed
- 2 pieces of garden hose or other flexible tubing, each approximately 6 feet (1.8 meters) long
- 1 large marble
- books, bricks, or wooden blocks
- masking tape
- chair
- tape measure or ruler

Approximate Budget
$20 if you need to buy a garden hose or other tubing.

Timetable
Approximately 2 hours.

Step-by-Step Instructions
1. To make the roller coaster track, lay the two pieces of garden hose or tubing side by side on a flat surface and tape them together across the upper side, so the tape does not show on the lower side. Place tape about every 6 inches (15 centimeters). Flip the taped hose or tubing over so the untaped side is up. The two pieces of hose should form a channel in which the marble can roll. (You can also form the roller coaster from a single uncut length of hose by making a sharp u-bend in the middle and taping the two halves together.)

How to Experiment Safely

Choose your experiment location carefully to avoid the marble rolling into places where it cannot be retrieved. Do not release the marble from very high heights, as it could jump off the roller coaster track and hit someone.

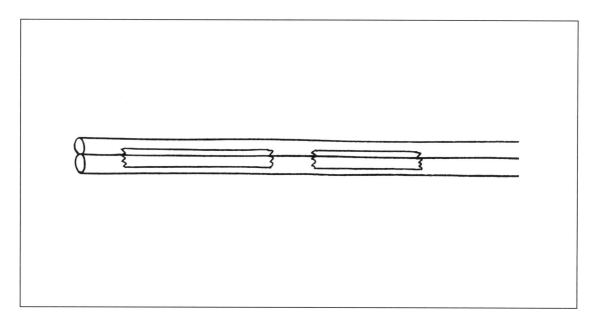

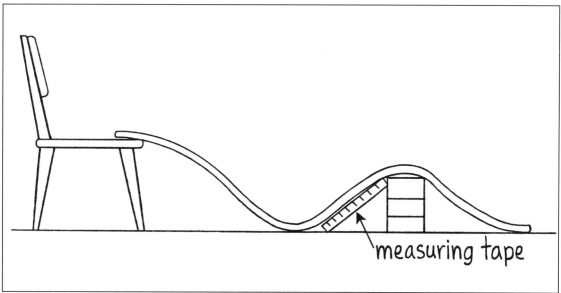

measuring tape

2. Place one end of the hose track on a chair 24 inches (60 centimeters) off the ground. Let the other end fall to the ground.

3. Let the hose track follow the ground for a short distance and then place two to three bricks under the other end, creating a second hill.

4. Record the height of both hills on a data sheet (see illustration on page 522). You have created your roller coaster.

TOP: Step 1: How to assemble roller coaster track.

BOTTOM: Steps 2 and 3: How to create the roller coaster.

Trial	First Hill Height	Height Rolled on Hill #2
1 (control)	2 feet	
2		
3		
4		
⋮		

Step 4: Recording chart for Experiment 2.

5. To make the heights easier to read, attach a tape measure or ruler vertically on the bricks that form the second hill. Be sure to put the "zero" end on the floor.

6. Place the marble at the top of the first hill and release it. Do not push it, but simply let it go. Sight across your tape measure or ruler to determine the height the marble reaches on the second hill. You might ask a friend to help you note the highest height before the marble begins to roll back again.

7. Repeat this procedure several times and record the average height the marble reaches on the second hill.

8. Now raise the height of the first hill by adding a book or block on the chair. Record the new height of the first hill.

9. Release the marble from the higher first hill several times, taking an average of the heights it reaches on the second hill. Record the average height.

10. Repeat the procedure, raising and lowering the height of the first hill. Be sure to record each hill height and the height the marble reaches on the second hill.

Summary of Results

Study the results on your chart. Compare the heights of the first hills and the heights the marble reached on the second hill. Did higher initial heights give your marble more potential energy, which created more kinetic energy to climb the second hill? Was your hypothesis correct? If you want to calculate the potential energy, use the formula described and record the number for each of your hill heights.

Change the Variables

You can vary this experiment several ways. For example, remember that potential energy depends partially on the weight of the object. Try using a heavier or lighter marble. What is the effect? You can also try making the second hill steeper or more gradual. What is the effect? How high does the marble rise? Make your first hill higher and create a number of smaller hills with your hose. Can you build up enough

 ## Troubleshooter's Guide

Below are some problems that may occur during this experiment, possible causes, and ways to remedy the problem.

Problem: The marble jumped over the second hill.

Possible causes:

1. Your second hill is not high enough. Use more blocks or bricks to make it higher. The height of the hill does not matter as long as you record the height the ball reaches accurately.

2. Your first hill is too high. Lower it until you can release the marble and it stays on the second hill.

Problem: The marble does not stay on the hose track.

Possible cause: The marble is too large or too small for the hose. Try using a different size marble that fits well into the track.

potential energy to get your marble over more than one hill? What conditions will allow the marble to do that?

 ## Design Your Own Experiment

How to Select a Topic Relating to this Concept

If you are interested in kinetic energy, you could explore the energy in vibrations, in rotational movement, or in objects moving in straight lines or up and down. Or you could investigate the use of kinetic energy in heat or electricity.

If you are interested in potential energy, you could study the effects of springs. How does the size or flexibility of the spring affect its potential energy? How much weight can a spring move? You could study the swing of a pendulum (using a backyard swing) as its potential energy is converted to kinetic energy and back again.

Check the For More Information section and talk with your science teacher or school or community media specialist to start gathering information on potential and kinetic energy questions that interest you. As you consider possible experiments, be sure to discuss them with your science teacher or other knowledgeable adult before trying them. Some might be dangerous.

Steps in the Scientific Method

To do an original experiment, you need to plan carefully and think things through before you do it. Otherwise you might not be sure what question you are answering, what you are or should be measuring, or what your findings prove or disprove.

Here are the steps in designing an experiment:

- State the purpose of—and underlying question behind—the experiment you propose to do.
- Recognize the variables involved, and select one that will help you answer the question at hand.
- State a testable hypothesis, an educated guess, about the answer to your question.
- Decide how to change the variable you selected.
- Decide how to measure your results.

Recording Data and Summarizing the Results

Your data should include charts, such as the one you did for these experiments. They should be clearly labeled and easy to read. You may also want to include photos, graphs, or drawings of your experimental setup and results. If you have done a nonexperimental project, explain clearly what your research question was and illustrate your findings.

Related Projects

Besides completing experiments, you could prepare a model that demonstrates a point you are interested in with regard to kinetic and potential energy. Or you could investigate the uses of energy in industry, cooking, music, medicine, or dancing. You could explore the history of the study of energy, going all the way back to Newton and Galileo, or you could look at the future of energy, exploring nuclear and fusion energy. There are numerous possibilities.

For More Information

Bennet, Bob, Dan Keen, Alex Pang, and Frances Zweifel. *Science Fair Projects: Energy.* New York: Sterling Publications, 1998. ❖ Simple activities and ideas about science fair projects related to energy and using simple materials.

Doherty, Paul, and Don Rathjen. *The Cool Hot Rod and Other Electrifying Experiments on Energy and Matter.* New York: John Wiley & Sons, 1996. ❖ Collection of twenty-two experiments on all aspects of energy, with drawings, photos, and sidebars.

Leary, Catherine, and Michael Anthony DiSpezio. *Awesome Experiments in Force & Motion.* New York: Sterling Publications, 1998. ❖ Provides exciting ideas for kinetic energy projects.

chapter 35

Rocks and Minerals

According to archaeologists (scientists who study the past remains of human activities), the Copper, Bronze, and Iron Ages were named for the main minerals that were being used in tools during those time periods, which spanned 10,000 B.C. to 2,000 B.C.. **Minerals** are natural, nonliving solids—tiny particles arranged in definite patterns. **Rocks** are solid mixtures of minerals. If you look at a rock with a magnifying lens, you can often see the distinct grains of several different minerals.

Earth is a living machine

At the end of the eighteenth century, James Hutton (1726–1797), a Scottish doctor, met once a week in Edinburgh to talk with other visionary men about new ideas. The Industrial Revolution was just beginning, and the men he met included James Watt, inventor of the steam engine, and Joseph Black, the chemist who discovered carbon dioxide. Hutton was interested in the rock and soil of his homeland and discussed his theories with this group.

Certain cliffs overlooking the North Sea, called Siccar Point, particularly fascinated Hutton. The upper part of the cliffs is red sandstone in horizontal layers, while the lower half is a dark rock tilted almost vertically. He knew the cliffs did not just magically appear in this form. After years of study, Hutton concluded that Earth was like a living machine, driven by heat within. He theorized that over thousands of centuries, the heated material within Earth's core erupted and formed deposits on the ocean bottom. Over time, these deposits rose to form new land. Then rains eroded them, sending some of the soil

Words to Know

Cleavage:
The tendency of a mineral to split along certain planes.

Crust:
The hard, outer shell of Earth that floats upon the softer, denser mantle.

Fracture:
A mineral's tendency to break into curved, rough, or jagged surfaces.

Geology:
The study of the origin, history and structure of Earth.

experiment
CENTRAL

Words to Know

Igneous rock:
Rock formed from the cooling and hardening of magma.

Inner core:
Very dense, solid center of Earth.

Lava:
Molten rock that occurs at the surface of Earth, usually through volcanic eruptions.

Luster:
A glow of reflected light; a sheen.

Mantle:
Thick, dense layer of rock that underlies Earth's crust and overlies the core.

Metamorphic rock:
Rock formed by transformation of pre-existing rock through changes in temperature and pressure.

Mineral:
An inorganic substance found in nature with a definite chemical composition and structure. Most have a crystal form.

and rock particles back into the oceans. It was part of a continual cycle of creation and destruction.

In 1788, Hutton presented his ideas to the Royal Society of Edinburgh. He was not entirely correct, but his theory was accepted at the time and represented the beginning of modern **geology,** the science of rocks, volcanoes, earthquakes, and the history of Earth.

Shake, rattle, and roll

Earth's very hot, solid **inner core** is the machine that Hutton envisioned. Earth's inner core is surrounded by an **outer core,** a hot layer of liquid metal. After that comes a layer called the **mantle,** which produces the liquid rock of volcanoes. Earth's **crust** is the top layer, the one on which we live.

Huge, moving blocks of rock called **plates** make up Earth's crust. Their fit is similar to the pieces of a cracked eggshell. The boundaries where the pieces meet are called **seismic belts.** Cracks along these belts allow heat from the upper mantle to escape. Within seismic belts, movement, heat, and eruptions combine to form various minerals, each kind with a specific crystal form. Some valuable minerals are located by mining near seismic belts.

Classifying this old rock

Rocks vary enormously because of the way they are formed. Geologists, scientists who study rocks, classify them into three categories: igneous, sedimentary, and metamorphic rocks. **Igneous** (pronounced IG-knee-us) rocks are formed when rock material cools from a hot, liquid state called **magma.** Magma is a thick substance like melted glass. When it reaches Earth's surface, usually through volcanic eruptions, it is called **lava.**

Sedimentary rocks are formed from particles that have broken away from other rocks and have been washed down and deposited on the bottoms of lakes or oceans. These particles may become mixed with fragments of dead plants or seashells. Over millions of years, these deposits may get buried under other rocks and soil. The pressure of tons of earth above the particles packs them together in layers and hardens them into rock.

The molten lava from this Hawaiian volcano is a form of rock that shot up from the depths of Earth's mantle. (Photo Researchers Inc. Reproduced by permission.)

experiment
CENTRAL

Metamorphic (pronounced meta-MORE-fic) rocks are formed from sedimentary and igneous rock that become deeply buried in Earth. They are not formed from melting. Instead, the combination of intense heat and pressure changes them into different minerals. Metamorphic, in fact, means "changed in shape."

When you think about it, Earth really is a living machine that forms the rocks and minerals that serve as the foundation of our daily lives. In the two projects that follow, you will examine rocks and minerals closely to learn more about them.

Project 1
Mineral Testing: What kind of mineral is it?

Purpose
In this project, you will determine the characteristics of mineral samples, such as hardness, luster, and color. Each mineral has specific characteristics, or properties, that distinguish it from other minerals and can help you identify it.

Level of Difficulty
Moderate/difficult.

Materials Needed
- white ceramic tile
- hammer
- magnifying lens
- glass plate or cup (used, since you will be scratching it as part of the experiment)
- penny
- 4 samples of unpolished minerals (gathered outdoors or purchased at a store; avoid polished samples because they lose some of their natural properties)
- 4 index cards
- goggles

Approximate Budget
Less than $10 for a tile, minerals, and a magnifying lens.

Timetable
20 minutes.

Words to Know

Outer core:
A liquid core that surrounds Earth's solid inner core; made mostly of iron.

Plates:
Large regions of Earth's surface, composed of the crust and uppermost mantle, which move about, forming many of Earth's major geologic surface features.

Rock:
Naturally occurring solid mixture of minerals.

Sedimentary rock:
Rock formed from the compressed and solidified layers of organic or inorganic matter.

Seismic belt:
Boundaries where Earth's plates meet.

Streak:
The color of the dust left when a mineral is rubbed across a rough surface.

OPPOSITE PAGE:
Mountains may include rocks of many types. (Photo Researchers Inc. Reproduced by permission.)

Step-by-Step Instructions

1. Prepare an index card, as illustrated, to record data for each of your samples.

2. Number each sample and write the same number on an index card.

3. Determine and record the color or colors of each sample.

4. Check the streak. The **streak** of a mineral is the color of the dust

TOP: Step 1: Index card set-up.

BOTTOM: Step 4: Using the underside of the ceramic tile, firmly rub the mineral across the tile.

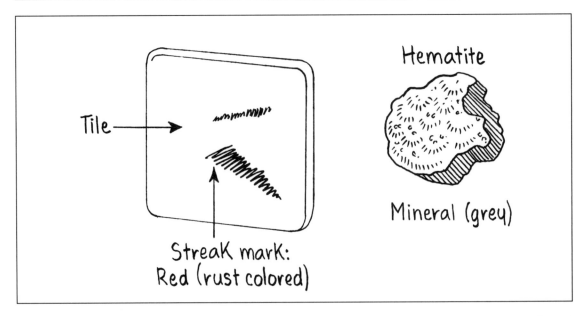

Mineral name: _____

Characteristics: _____

Color: _____   Luster: _____
Streak: _____   Cleavage:
                          (Draw fragment)

Hardness: _____

Special properties: _____

Tile →

Streak mark:
Red (rust colored)

Hematite

Mineral (grey)

How to Work Safely

Wear goggles at all times when testing minerals. Mineral fragments and dust can irritate your eyes.

left when the mineral is rubbed across a rough surface. Using the underside of the ceramic tile, firmly rub the mineral across the tile. Record the color of any residue left on the tile.

5. Examine the **luster** or shine of the mineral. If the mineral is shiny gold, silver, or grey, it is considered metallic. If it is not shiny, it is considered nonmetallic. Describe the luster of each mineral (metallic or nonmetallic) on its card.

6. Determine how each mineral breaks apart when struck. **Cleavage** is a mineral's tendency to break in along smooth, flat planes. **Fracture** is a mineral's tendency to break into curved, rough, or jagged surfaces. Wearing your goggles, strike the mineral with a hammer and break it. Using the magnifying lens, observe how many flat surfaces exist on the broken pieces. Draw your findings on the data card.

Step 6: Determine how each mineral breaks apart when struck. Wear your goggles!

rock hammer

Halite

mineral sample

magnifying glass

WEAR GOGGLES!

7. Check each mineral's hardness, using the Moh's Hardness Scale, shown below. The scale ranges from 1 (softest mineral, such as talc) to 10 (hardest mineral, such as a diamond). To determine the hardness of each mineral, see what it scratches.

If it:	Moh's Hardness Scale
Scratches glass	5.5–5.6
Scratches a penny, but does not scratch glass	3.5–5.5
Scratches a fingernail, but does not scratch a penny or glass	2.5–3.5
Does not scratch a fingernail, penny, or glass	1.0–2.5

8. Some minerals have special properties, such as being magnetic or dissolving in water. Some have a different smell, taste funny, react with acid, or glow under ultraviolet light. If you notice any special properties for each mineral, record them on its card.

Summary of Results

Compare your results. What colors were your samples? Did the color of the streaks surprise you because they were different from the mineral? Could you tell if the samples were metallic or nonmetallic? How did the samples compare in hardness? If you wish, use a mineral identification guide and the properties you identified to determine the name of each sample. Set up a display of your samples and their data cards.

Project 2
Rock Classification: Is it igneous, sedimentary, or metamorphic?

Purpose

This project will give you the basic knowledge needed to classify igneous, sedimentary, and metamorphic rocks.

Level of Difficulty

Moderate.

How to Work Safely
Wear goggles at all times and use the hammer outside, away from others.

Materials Needed
- hammer
- 12 rock samples of different colors, sizes, and textures.
- flat, hard surface—old table or board
- egg carton
- permanent marking pen
- goggles
- magnifying lens

Approximate Budget
$0. If possible, gather rock samples outdoors and borrow a hammer and goggles. Other materials should be available in the average household.

Timetable
1 hour.

Step-by-Step Instructions
1. Using the hammer outside on the table or board, carefully crack each rock sample to expose a fresh surface.

2. Place a sample of each rock into the egg carton wells.

3. Use the marking pen to label each sample with a number from 1 to 12.

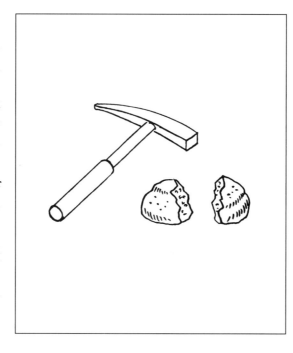

Step 1: Carefully crack each rock sample with the hammer to expose a fresh surface.

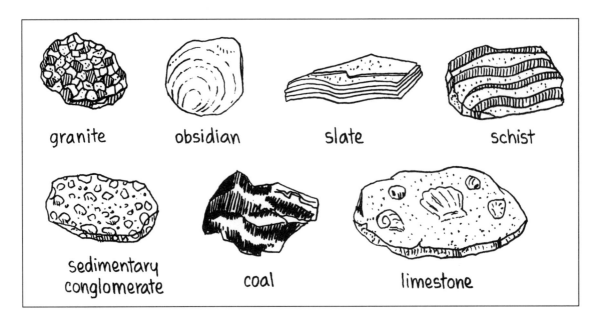

granite   obsidian   slate   schist

sedimentary
conglomerate   coal   limestone

Step 5: Examples of igneous, metamorphic, and sedimentary rocks.

4. Construct a data sheet to log all observations (see illustration).

5. Using a magnifying lens, examine each rock. Look for characteristics such as:

Troubleshooter's Guide

Here are some problems that may arise during this experiment, some possible causes, and ways to remedy the problems.

Problem: You cannot see any visible characteristics in some of the samples.

Possible cause: Some samples may be too small. A larger sample may be needed. For example, layers in metamorphic rock may be hard to see in a small sample.

Problem: A sample seems to possess properties of two groups, such as metamorphic layers and sand grains.

Possible cause: Since metamorphic rock is derived from other types of rocks, a sample may possess properties from other categories.

Sample #	Observation/Characteristics	Check one
		I M S
1		☐ ☐ ☐
2		☐ ☐ ☐
3		☐ ☐ ☐
4		☐ ☐ ☐
5		☐ ☐ ☐
6		☐ ☐ ☐
7		☐ ☐ ☐
8		☐ ☐ ☐
9		☐ ☐ ☐
10		☐ ☐ ☐
11		☐ ☐ ☐
12		☐ ☐ ☐

Data sheet for Project 2.

- Igneous rocks (formed from cooled, liquid rock): Contain large or small crystals; appears glassy with seashell pattern when cracked.

- Metamorphic rocks (derived from pre-existing rock that was changed by heat and pressure): Layers that appear wavy.

- Sedimentary rocks (formed from pre-existing rock fragments or seashells or dead plants or animals): Include fossils—preserved plant or animal remains; contains pebbles, sand, silt, or clay particles; contains carbon or coal; contains layers.

Summary of Results

Examine your data sheet. Based on the visible properties, place each rock in one of the three categories. Remember, you must see some evidence to justify your conclusion. For example, sample 3 in the illustration, fossilized limestone, has sand grains as well as small seashell fragments, so it must be sedimentary rock.

Design Your Own Experiment

How to Select a Topic Relating to this Concept

Rocks and minerals are present in your daily life, from the rocks in the cement of our sidewalks to the minerals in bath powder. Choose a type of rock or mineral to study. Minerals used in household cleaning and rocks used in industry are just two leads you can investigate.

Check the For More Information section and talk with your science teacher or school or community media specialist to gather information on rock and mineral questions that interest you. As you consider possible experiments, be sure to discuss them with a knowledgeable adult before trying them.

Steps in the Scientific Method

To do an original experiment, you need to plan carefully and think things through. Otherwise, you might not be sure what question you are answering, what you are or should be measuring, or what your findings prove or disprove.

Here are the steps in designing an experiment:

- State the purpose of—and the underlying question behind—the experiment you propose to do.
- Recognize the variables involved, and select one that will help you answer the question at hand.
- State a testable hypothesis, an educated guess about the answer to your question.
- Decide how to change the variable you selected.
- Decide how to measure your results.

Recording Data and Summarizing the Results

Make drawings, graphs, and charts to display your information for others. You might also draw conclusions about your findings. Which minerals seem to be the most common in your region? Why might that be?

Related Projects

If you are interested in rocks and minerals and want to discover more of their uses in your daily life, you might investigate how rocks are used to prevent erosion or what consistency is the best for plaster, whose main ingredient is minerals. The possibilities are almost as endless as our supply of rocks and minerals.

For More Information

Barrow, Lloyd H. *Adventures with Rocks and Minerals.* Hillside, NJ: Enslow Publishing, 1991. ❖ Describes geological experiments. Chapters include what causes minerals to break and what freezing does to rocks.

Cox, Shirley. *Earth Science.* Vero Beach, FL: Rourke Publications, Inc., 1992. ❖ Chapters include how to choose geology projects.

Knapp, Brian. *Mountain.* Danbury, CT: Grolier, 1992. ❖ Describes mountains and their makeup. Some chapters include experiments.

Parker, Steve. *The Earth.* North Bellmore, NY: Marshall Cavendish, 1993. ❖ Outlines a variety of projects and experiments that examine Earth's composition.

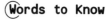

chapter 36

Salinity

What gives ocean water its salty taste? The answer lies in its **salinity,** the total salt content of the water. Saline (salty) substances are present in all water, even rain water, but sodium and chlorine are the two most abundant saline substances dissolved in ocean water.

Get out the yardstick

In 1872, the H.M.S. *Challenger* began its worldwide ocean expedition from Portsmouth, England. On board were 240 sailors and scientists, including four naturalists and their support team. Originally built as a warship, the ship was converted into a floating scientific lab by the British government to study the biology of the sea, as well as the chemical and physical properties of the water. Between 1872 and 1876, the ship sailed 68,890 miles (110,908 kilometers) and made 492 stops. Nearly 5,000 new species, including giant worms and deep-sea shrimp almost as big as lobsters, were brought on board and identified.

Samples of seawater were also collected and analyzed for their chemical composition. The main substances present included bicarbonates and sulfates, as well as salts such as calcium, magnesium, potassium, sodium, and chloride. Sodium and chloride were the most abundant. While the samples showed that different salinity measurements existed, the average salinity of all the samples was about 3.5 percent, or 35 pounds (kilograms) of salt per 1,000 pounds (kilograms) of seawater. Scientists today still use this average salinity figure, and the *Challenger's* salinity samples are still the only worldwide set of analyzed seawater. In fact, this voyage helped launch modern **oceanography.** John Murray,

Words to Know

Buoyancy:
The upward force exerted on an object placed in a liquid.

Calibration:
To standardize or adjust a measuring instrument so its measurements are correct.

Density:
The mass of a substance compared to its volume.

Density ball:
A ball with the fixed standard of 1.0 gram per milliliter, which is the exact density of pure water.

In 1872, the crew of the H.M.S. Challenger *were the first to measure ocean salinity. (North Wind Picture Archive. Reproduced by permission.)*

one of naturalists onboard, later supervised the publication of fifty volumes of *Challenger Reports* based on the expedition's discoveries.

Where did the salt come from?

Millions of years ago, one ocean covered Earth. This vast ocean was just barely salty. Over time, land formed, and rain washed salt and minerals from the land into the ocean. Salt also came from rocks and sediments on the ocean floor, and from undersea volcanic activity that literally erupted salts into the water. All these accumulated salts made ocean water heavier, that is, gave it a greater **density** than fresh water.

The discoveries made on the *Challenger* gave us an average salinity for oceans, but this number can vary quite a bit. For example, the Baltic Sea near Sweden has a salinity content of 1 percent; while the Red Sea near Egypt has a salinity content of 27 percent. Salinity increases through evaporation, which begins as the surface water of the

Words to Know

Hydrometer:
An instrument that determines the specific gravity of a liquid.

Hypothesis:
An idea in the form of a statement that can be tested by observation and/or experiment.

The Red Sea has a salinity level of 27 percent. (Peter Arnold Inc. Reproduced by permission.)

ocean is warmed by the Sun. The heated water becomes water vapor and rises into the atmosphere, leaving the salt behind.

Generally, waters in climates with strong sunlight and high temperatures, such as the region around the Red Sea, tend to have a higher salinity level because the surface water there evaporates at a faster rate. In the Baltic Sea region, rain, fresh water from adjoining rivers, and melting ice keep the salinity level low. The colder weather there also reduces the evaporation rate.

Getting the evidence

Two instruments used to analyze ocean water are **hydrometers,** which measure seawater density, and Nansen bottles. Nansen bottles are more sophisticated versions of those collection bottles used on the H.M.S. *Challenger.* The bottles are self-closing containers with thermometers; they can draw in water at different depths. Through their use, scien-

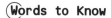
Words to Know

Nansen bottles:
Self-closing containers with thermometers that draw in water at different depths.

Oceanography:
The study of the chemistry of the oceans, as well as their currents, marine life, and the ocean bed.

Nansen bottles are used to take seawater samples. (Elizabeth Venrick. Reproduced by permission.)

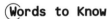ords to Know

Salinity:
The amount of salts dissolved in water.

Specific gravity:
The ratio of the density of a substance to the density of pure water.

Standard:
A base for comparison.

Variable:
Something that can affect the results of an experiment.

tists have learned that the sea has different layers of water with specific salinity levels and temperatures.

In the two experiments that follow, you will learn more about salinity by measuring it in different ways.

Experiment 1
Making a Hydrometer: How can salinity be measured?

Purpose/Hypothesis
In this experiment, you will create a scientific instrument called a hydrometer. A hydrometer is used to measure the **specific gravity** of water, comparing the density of one water sample to that of pure water. Pure water has a density of 1.000 grams/milliliter. If any salts or chemicals are added, they will dissolve and their added mass will

increase the density of the water. This will increase the specific gravity. The greater the specific gravity, the greater the salinity.

A hydrometer works on the Archimedes Principle of **buoyancy,** which states that a liquid exerts an upward buoyant force on an object equal to the amount of liquid displaced by the object. Thus if an object floats partially submerged in water, the downward weight of the object must be counterbalanced by the upward buoyant force, which is equal to the weight of the water displaced. Otherwise, the object would sink to the bottom.

If you add salt to the water, the downward weight of the object will displace less water because the water is now denser—that is, it has more mass for a given volume. As a result, the object will float higher in the water, with less of it submerged. If you place measurement graduations along the surface of the object where the water touches, you have created a hydrometer. The hydrometer measurements can then be equated to the specific gravity, and in turn to the amount of salt in the water, or salinity.

To begin the experiment, use what you have learned about salinity to make a guess about what will happen to the specific gravity of water when salt is added. This educated guess is your **hypothesis.** A hypothesis should explain these things:

What Are the Variables?

Variables are anything that might affect the results of an experiment. Here are the main variables in this experiment:

- the amount of water in the sample
- the amount of salt in the water
- the temperature of the water
- the accuracy of the hydrometer measurements

In other words, the variables in this experiment are everything that might affect the specific gravity of the water. If you change more than one variable at a time, you will not be able to determine which variable had the most effect on the specific gravity.

- the topic of the experiment
- the **variable** you will change
- the variable you will measure
- what you expect to happen

A hypothesis should be brief, specific, and measurable. It must be something you can test through observation. Your experiment will prove or disprove whether your hypothesis is correct. Here is one possible hypothesis for this experiment: "The more salt in the water, the higher its specific gravity."

In this case, the variable you will change is the amount of salt in the water, and the variable you will measure is the water's specific gravity. If the specific gravity increases with an increase in salt, your hypothesis is correct.

Level of Difficulty

Moderate/difficult because accurate measurements and adjustments are required.

Materials Needed

- one 1-quart (1-liter) graduated cylinder filled with distilled water at room temperature
- one 5-inch (12.7-centimeter) test tube
- one 6-inch (15.2-centimeter) glass rod

Materials for Experiment 1.

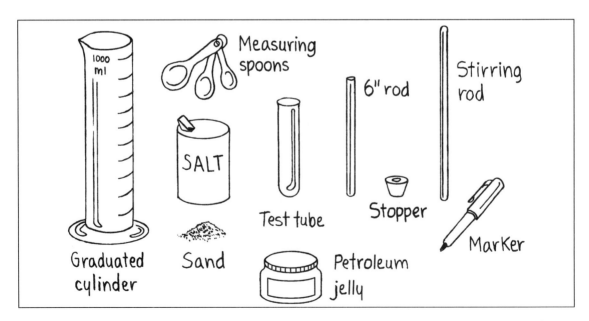

- 1 rubber test tube stopper with a single hole that fits the glass rod
- 2 tablespoons (30 milliliters) sand
- 1 to 3 cups (250 to 750 milliliters) table salt
- small amount of petroleum jelly
- fine tip permanent marker
- measuring spoons
- stirring rod

Approximate Budget

$0 to $10. Ideally, you can borrow most of the materials from school. Ask your science teacher for help.

Timetable

About 1 hour.

Step-by-Step Instructions

1. Place a small dab of petroleum jelly on the end of the glass rod. Push the glass rod through the stopper until it reaches the bottom of the stopper.

2. Place a pinch or two of sand into the test tube and place the stopper into it. You have made a hydrometer.

3. Place the test tube hydrometer into the graduated cylinder of distilled water.

4. Add or remove some of the sand from the test tube until the hydrometer floats vertically in the water with approximately 1 inch (2.5 centimeters) of the glass rod above the water.

5. Use the marker to write 1.000 on the glass rod at the level of the surface of the water.

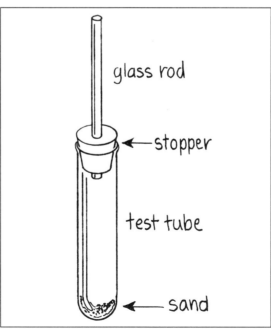

glass rod

←stopper

test tube

←sand

Steps 1 and 2: Making a hydrometer.

Steps 3 to 8: Hydrometer in graduated cylinder of distilled water with different water levels marked.

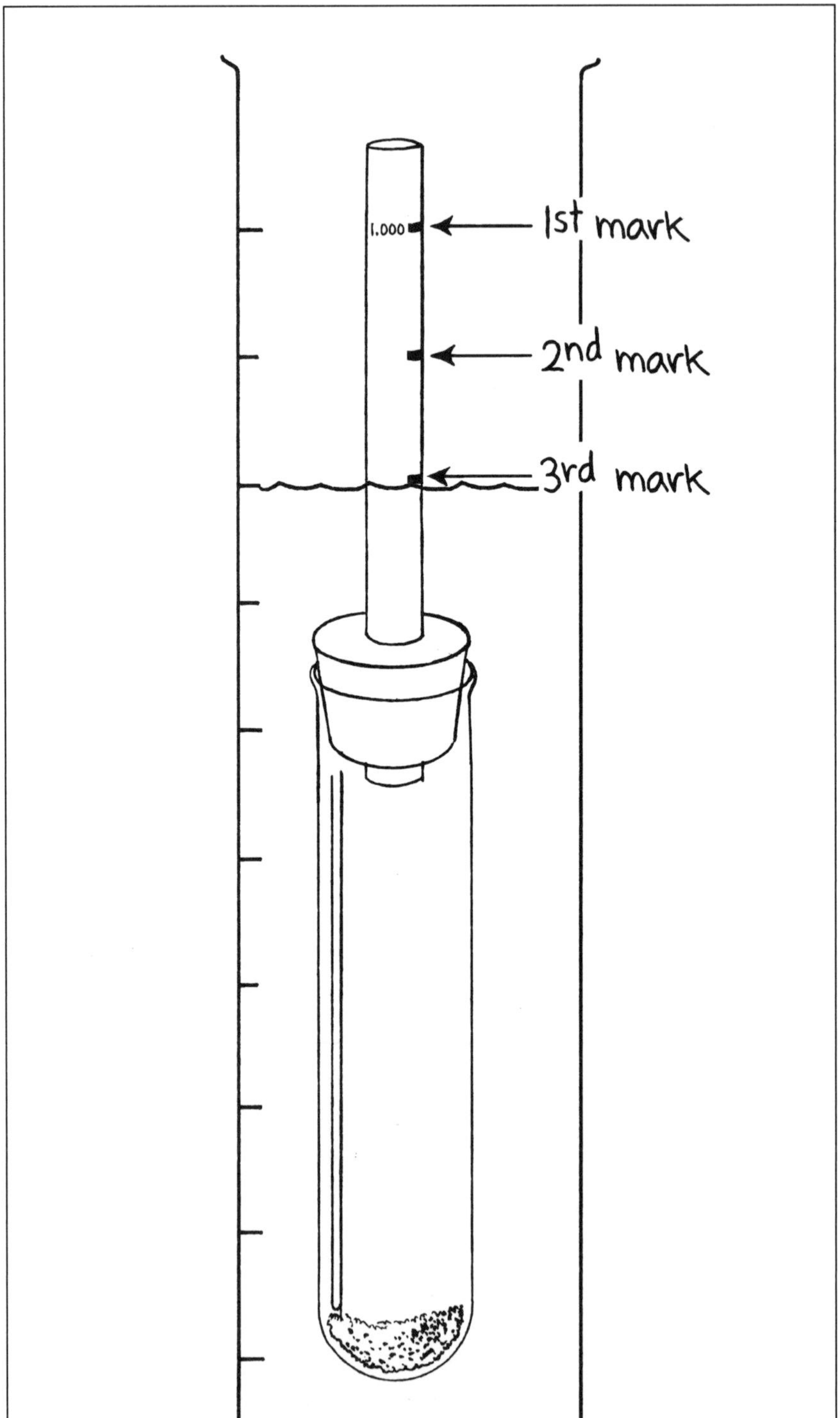

1.000 ← 1st mark

← 2nd mark

← 3rd mark

experiment
CENTRAL

How to Experiment Safely

Be sure to handle glass carefully.

6. Remove the hydrometer from the water and stir in 3 tablespoons of salt. This is equivalent to about 3.5 ounces (100 grams) of salt. Stir until all of the salt is dissolved.

7. Place the hydrometer in the water and mark the new water level. It should be lower on the rod because the water is denser and the hydrometer is now floating slightly higher. The increased water density, compared to the density of pure water, means the salty water has a higher specific gravity.

8. Add another 3 tablespoons of salt and mark the water level again. The hydrometer should float even higher in the water as the density (and specific gravity) of the water increases.

Summary of Results

Study the marks on your hydrometer. Do they support your hypothesis? Did the specific gravity increase each time you added more salt to the water? What does this tell you about the salinity of the water? Write a paragraph describing and explaining your results.

Troubleshooter's Guide

Below is a problem that may arise during this experiment, a possible cause, and a way to remedy the situation.

Problem: The test tube does not float vertically in the water.

Possible cause: There is not enough weight in the bottom of the tube to keep it upright. Use more sand or substitute a denser material instead of sand, such as small roller bearings.

Change the Variables

You can change the variables in this experiment in several ways. For example, you can chill the water by placing it in a refrigerator to determine the effect of water temperature on salinity. You could also use a different kind of salt—for example, potassium chloride instead of sodium chloride.

Experiment 2
Density Ball: How to make a standard for measuring density

Purpose/Hypothesis

This experiment is designed to create a **standard**. A standard is an object or instrument that has a fixed value. In this experiment, you will create a standard for measuring the density of a solution, called a **density ball**. A density ball has the fixed standard of 1.0 gram/milliliter, which is the exact density of pure water. You will then determine if your standard can accurately indicate if a water sample's density is greater than or equal to pure water.

This experiment is similar to Experiment #1, except here you will determine density by watching whether the density ball standard is suspended or floats.

To begin the experiment, use what you know about the density of pure water to make an educated guess about how a density ball will work. This educated guess, or prediction, is your **hypothesis**. A hypothesis should explain these things:

- the topic of the experiment
- the **variable** you will change
- the variable you will measure
- what you expect to happen

A hypothesis should be brief, specific, and measurable. It must be something you can test through observation. Your experiment will prove or disprove whether your hypothesis is correct. Here is one possible hypothesis for this experiment: "By creating a standard for the density of pure water, you will be able to determine whether a solution has a density greater than or equal to 1.0 gram/milliliter."

What are the Variables

Variables are anything that might affect the results of an experiment. Here are the main variables in this experiment:

- the amount of water in the sample

- the amount of salt in the water

- the temperature of the water

- the behavior of the density ball

In other words, the variables in this experiment are everything that might affect the density reading indicated by the density ball. If you change more than one variable, you will not be able to determine which variable had the most effect on the density reading.

In this case, the variable you will change is the amount of salt in the water, and the variable you will measure is how your density ball reacts to changes in density. If your density ball accurately predicts whether a water sample is greater than or equal to the density of pure water, you will know your hypothesis is correct.

Level of Difficulty

Moderate, because delicate adjustments are required for this experiment.

Materials Needed

- one 1-quart (1-liter) graduated cylinder filled with distilled water at room temperature
- one 5-inch (12.7-centimeter) test tube
- 1 rubber test tube stopper without a hole
- 2 tablespoons (30 milliliters) sand
- 1 to 2 cups (250 to 500 milliliters) salt
- measuring spoons
- stirring rod

Approximate Budget

$0 to $10. See if you can borrow the lab materials from your science teacher. You probably have salt and perhaps sand at home.

Materials for Experiment 2.

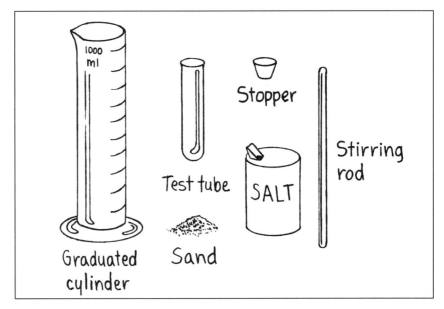

Timetable

30 minutes.

Step-by-Step Instructions

1. Place a pinch or two of sand in the test tube.

2. Place the stopper in the opening of the test tube securely. This is your density ball.

3. Place the test tube into the graduated cylinder of distilled water.

4. Wait 15 to 20 seconds and note where the test tube is positioned. If it is suspended freely in the water without floating to the surface or sinking to the bottom, it has the same density as water at room temperature: 1.0 gram/milliliter. If the test tube sinks to the bottom, remove some sand and try again. If it floats to the surface, add some sand.

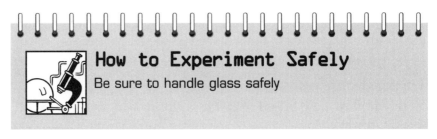

How to Experiment Safely

Be sure to handle glass safely

Freely suspended
in the water

Density ball = 1.0 g/ml

Step 4: Test tube freely suspended in water.

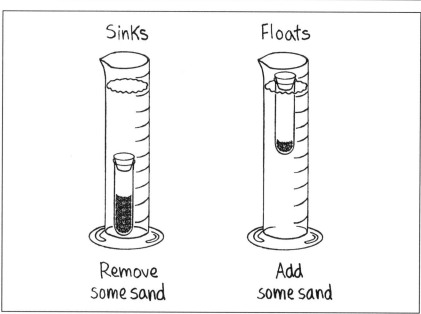

Sinks

Floats

Remove
some sand

Add
some sand

Step 4: What to do if test tube sinks to bottom or floats to surface.

5. Remove the test tube and stir 3 tablespoons—about 3.5 ounces (100 grams)— of salt into the water.

6. Place the test tube back into the water and note its position. (It should float now because the added salt makes the water denser than the ball.)

Troubleshooter's Guide

Below are some problems that may arise during this experiment, some possible causes, and ways to remedy the problems.

Problem: The test tube sinks and rests on the bottom.

Possible cause: The test tube is too heavy. Remove a pinch of sand from it and try again.

Problem: The test tube floats at the surface.

Possible cause: The test tube is not heavy enough. Add a pinch more sand and try again.

Summary of Results

Did your density ball indicate the density of the water and support your hypothesis? Write a paragraph explaining what you have learned during this experiment. How did your density ball behave in different solutions? What does this tell you about the solutions?

Change the Variables

You can change the variables and conduct other similar experiments. For example, try your 1.0 grams/milliliter standard density ball in another liquid, such as corn oil or vinegar, to determine if those liquids are more or less dense than pure water. How is the density of these liquids affected if you add salt?

Design Your Own Experiment

How to Select a Topic Relating to this Concept

If you are interested in salinity or its effects, there are many fascinating experiments you can explore. For example, how is salt used in the human body? Why does salt cause metal corrosion? How do marine animals adapt to their environment? These are all possible questions you can explore.

Check the For More Information section and talk with your science teacher or school or community media specialist to start gathering information on salinity questions that interest you. As you consider possible experiments, be sure to discuss them with your science teacher or another knowledgeable adult before trying them. Some of the materials or procedures might be dangerous.

Steps in the Scientific Method

To do an original experiment, you need to plan carefully and think things through. Otherwise, you might not be sure what question you are answering, what you are or should be measuring, or what your findings prove or disprove.

Here are the steps in designing an experiment:

- State the purpose of—and the underlying question behind—the experiment you propose to do.
- Recognize the variables involved and select one that will help you answer the question.
- State a testable hypothesis, an educated guess about the answer to your question.
- Decide how to change the variable you selected.
- Decide how to measure your results.

Recording Data and Summarizing the Results

Your data should include charts that are labeled and easy to read. You may also want to include photos, graphs, and drawings of your set-up and results. When working with salinity, you may be able to set up your experiment as a demonstration model. Do not forget to share what you have learned about salinity.

Related Projects

You might do an experiment on how salinity affects plants. Another possibility is to find the corrosion rate on metals exposed to salts. You may also want to explore the use of salts in chemistry and manufacturing. Be sure to talk with your teacher before starting a project.

For More Information

Lambert, David. *The Kingfisher Young People's Book of Oceans.* New York: Kingfisher, 1997. ❖ Includes nine ocean topics with related subjects. Describes how the oceans formed and the composition of seawater.

Rothaus, Don P. *Oceans.* Chanhassen, MN: The Child's World Inc., 1997. ❖ Describes the characteristics of the world's oceans including the chemistry of seawater.

chapter 37

Scientific Method

When you encounter a problem, how do you solve it? Do you consider what you already know about the problem, think of a possible answer, and then see if your answer is correct? If so, you are using the scientific method. The **scientific method** is a way of carefully collecting evidence about a question or problem, using that evidence to form a possible answer, and then testing the answer to see if it is accurate.

You can use this method as a tool for solving problems in science class and in many other areas of your life. For example, it could help you figure out why your pencils keep disappearing, how to wrap your sandwich so it does not dry out by lunchtime, or why your dog no longer likes his favorite food.

What are the steps in the scientific method?

The scientific method has six steps, described below. They will help you solve all kinds of problems, in and out of school.

- Step 1: State a problem or ask a question.
- Step 2: Gather background information.
- Step 3: Form a hypothesis.
- Step 4: Design and perform an experiment.
- Step 5: Draw a conclusion.
- Step 6: Report the results.

Step 1: State a problem or ask a question. To begin using the scientific method, think about the world around you. You may see something that makes you curious, such your sandwich drying out by

Words to Know

Control experiment:
A set-up that is identical to the experiment but is not affected by the variable that affects the experimental group.

Dependent variable:
The variable in an experiment whose value depends on the value of another variable in the experiment.

Experiment:
A controlled observation.

Hypothesis:
An idea phrased in the form of a statement that can be tested by observation and/or experiment.

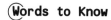

You do not have to be a scientist to use the scientific method. (Photo Researchers Inc. Reproduced by permission.)

lunchtime on some days but not on others. You might see an unexplained light in the sky. You might hear a statement that you are not sure is true. For example, a friend might tell you that wearing glasses makes your eyes become weaker.

Put your curiosity into the form of a problem or question, such as these:

- Why does my sandwich dry out some days but not others?
- What is that light in the sky?
- Does wearing glasses make your eyes weaker?

Step 2: Gather background information. Read more about the problem or question. Observe it closely.

Step 3: Form a hypothesis. Now use what you know about the situation to think of a possible answer for your question. This answer, or guess, is your hypothesis. A **hypothesis** is an idea in the form of a statement that can be tested by observations and/or experiment. You will use what you already know about the situation to form a hypothesis. Here are possible hypotheses to answer the questions above:

- Plastic bags that seal keep more moisture in bread than waxed paper or plastic bags without seals do.
- That light in the sky is an airplane.
- Wearing glasses does not make your eyes become weaker.

All of these hypothesis are testable: You can make observations, do research, or set up experiments to determine whether each hypothesis is correct. Here are some examples of hypotheses that are vague and untestable:

- Sandwiches taste better when you seal them in plastic bags. *How can you measure "taste better"?*
- The light in the sky might be a reflection or something. *How can you measure "might be" or "something"?*
- Wearing glasses might make your eyes weaker, if you wear them long enough. *How long is "long enough"?*

The ancient Greeks often hypothesized about the causes of natural events. However, they assumed they could figure out the correct explanations just by thinking about the situation long enough. They usually did not experiment to find out whether their explanations were accurate. Aristotle, a famous Greek philosopher, developed theories

Is the light in the sky just an airplane—or something else? (Photo Researchers Inc. Reproduced by permission.)

that led to many discoveries, but his theories were based mostly on reasoning, not experimentation. For example, he hypothesized that the flies that he found on rotting fruit just appeared out of the air. He did not experiment to find out whether his hypothesis was true.

Step 4: Design and perform an experiment. In this step, you go beyond the ancient Greeks: you prove or disprove your hypothesis. You might be able to establish whether your hypothesis is accurate by research, such as checking the local airport to see if an airplane flew over your house at a certain time last night. Or you might gather expert opinions about how wearing glasses affects people's eyesight. For the sandwich problem, the best approach is an experiment.

An **experiment** is a controlled observation. The experimenter carefully changes one condition at a time, such as the type of sandwich wrapping, and observes what happens. In most experiments, a **control experiment** is set up with the same conditions as the actual experiment. The conditions remain the same in the control experiment but are changed in the actual experiment, one condition at a time. If something happens only in the actual experiment and not in the control, it is clear that it was caused by changing a condition in the actual experiment. The control experiment for our sandwiches might be leaving a slice of bread unwrapped to see what happens to it and comparing it to those in various wrappings.

Conditions that change during an experiment and affect the results are called **variables.** The variables in our sample experiment include the type of bread, how fresh it is, the size of the piece of bread being wrapped, any fillings used with the bread, the length of time the bread is wrapped, the temperature of the wrapped bread during the experiment, and the type of sandwich wrapping. Only one variable is changed at a time during the experiment. The variable being changed is called the **independent variable,** which in our experiment is the type of sandwich wrapping.

What might happen if we change two variables at a time, such as wrapping wheat bread with waxed paper and putting rye bread in a sealed plastic bag? If the rye bread is fresher than the wheat bread at the end of the experiment, we cannot be sure which variable is the cause—the type of bread or the type of wrapping.

The condition that changes during an experiment is called the **dependent variable.** In our example, the dependent variable is the

amount of moisture in the bread. Results of experiments must be measurable, so we need a way to measure this moisture. We decide to weigh each slice of bread before and after the experiment. The difference in the weight would be the amount of moisture that evaporated.

Experiments must also be repeatable. We must write down our procedure and follow it carefully, so that someone else could carry out the same procedure and see if the same results occur.

Step 5: Draw a conclusion. The next step in the scientific method is to graph or chart our results, analyze them, and determine whether our hypothesis was correct. For some experiments, we might have quite a bit of data to analyze. For our sample experiment, we compare the loss in weight of each bread slice after the wrapping is removed. What is our conclusion? Did our results support our hypothesis?

Even if the results did not support our hypothesis, we have learned something just by asking the question and doing the experiment. Often there is no "right" answer when we use the scientific method. Instead, we simply gather more information about the problem, which is valuable in itself.

Step 6: Report the results. Reporting our results allows other scientists to build on our work—and to repeat our experiment to see if they get the same results. Without the sharing of results, little scientific progress would be made. Scientists publish their findings in scientific journals as a way of sharing what they have learned.

In the two experiments that follow, you will use information you gather to identify mystery powders, and you will use the scientific method to prove or disprove Aristotle's hypothesis that fruit flies appear out of thin air.

Experiment 1
Using the Scientific Method: What are the mystery powders?

Purpose/Hypothesis

In this experiment, you will begin with three mystery powders and ask yourself, "What are these powders?" Then you will gather information from a chart that shows how three kinds of powder react when mixed with water, iodine, and vinegar. Next, you will hypothesize the identity of each mystery powder. Then you will test how each powder reacts with water, iodine, and vinegar. You will compare your results with the chart and draw a conclusion about the identity of each powder. Then you will know whether your hypothesis was correct.

A hypothesis should explain these things:

What Are the Variables?

Variables are anything that might affect the results of an experiment. Here are the main variables in this experiment:

- the purity of the sample of each powder
- the amount of water, iodine, and vinegar that is added to each powder
- the accuracy of your observations

In other words, the variables in this experiment are everything that might affect how each powder reacts to the water, iodine, and vinegar.

- the topic of the experiment
- the variable you will change
- the variable you will measure
- what you expect to happen

A hypothesis should be brief, specific, and measurable. It must be something you can test through observation. Your experiment will prove or disprove whether your hypothesis is correct.

Level of Difficulty

Easy/moderate.

Materials Needed

- 3 ounces (85 grams) each of these powders in their original containers:
    baking soda
    cornstarch
    flour
- 6 small labels
- 6 small dishes
- 3 spoons
- water
- iodine (the kind used to prevent infections)
- vinegar
- eye dropper
- black paper
- magnifying lens
- goggles or other eye protection

Approximate Budget

Up to $10; most materials available in the average household.

Timetable

Approximately 30 minutes.

Step-by-Step Instructions

1. Turn three of the small dishes upside down and attach a label to each bottom that says *baking soda, cornstarch,* or *flour.*

2. Turn the three dishes right side up.

3. Put about 3 oz. (85 g) of the powder on the label (baking soda, cornstarch, or flour) into each dish. Make sure the amounts are

How to Experiment Safely

Wear goggles to prevent the iodine, vinegar, or any of the powders from getting in your eyes. *Never* taste substances you are using in an experiment.

equal. After the dishes are filled, you should no longer be able to read the labels on the bottom.

4. Move the dishes around until you no longer know which powder is which. (You might ask another person to do this while you wait in another room.)

Step 6: Table 1, Characteristics of Three Powders

5. Add a label to the side of each dish that says *A, B,* or *C.*

Table 1
Characteristics of Three Powders

Powder	Appearance or feel	Reaction with water	Reaction with iodine	Reaction with vinegar
baking soda	powdery	slowly dissolves	none	bubbles or fizzes
cornstarch	silky smooth	turns cloudy	turns black	none
flour	gritty	turns cloudy	turns black	none

experiment
CENTRAL

Table 2
Chart of Reactions

Powder	Appearance or feel	Reaction with water	Reaction with iodine	Reaction with vinegar
A				
B				
C				

6. Gather information by studying Table 1 (see illustration). Notice how each powder looks or feels and how it reacts with water, iodine, and vinegar. Iodine will turn a powder black if the powder contains starch. Vinegar, an acid, will make a powder bubble or fizz if the powder is a base. The acid and base react with each other to produce carbon dioxide.

7. Create a table similar to the one illustrated above. You will fill in the table as you test each powder.

8. Pour a small amount of Powder A on the black paper, and carefully observe it with the magnifying lens. Repeat with Powders B and C. Do you notice any slight variations in color or any other differences? Add your observations to Table 2.

9. Feel each powder, rinsing your hands after touching each one. Record your observations on Table 2.

Step 7: Create a Chart of Reactions for Experiment 1.

Step 15: Add 1 to 2 drops of iodine to Powder A.

10. Based on your observations, make a hypothesis about the identities of Powders A, B, and C. Remember that a hypothesis is a clear, testable statement of your educated guess about the identity of the unknown powders. Here is a possible hypothesis: "Powder A is baking soda. Powder B is flour. Powder C is cornstarch."

11. Fill an empty dish with about 2 oz. (60 ml) of water. Add about 1/2 ounce (14 gr) of Powder A and stir with a spoon. Notice whether the powder dissolves in the water and the water remains clear, or whether the powder does not dissolve and the water becomes cloudy. Record your observations in Table 2.

12. Throw away the powder sample you just tested. Rinse and dry the spoon and small dish. Use the same spoon and dish each time you test Powder A.

13. Repeat Steps 11 and 12 with Powder B and Powder C, using the other two dishes. Record your observations.

14. Place about 1/2 ounce (14 gr) of Powder A into its empty dish.

15. Use the eye dropper to add 1 to 2 drops of iodine to Powder A. Observe what happens and record the results in your table. If Powder A contains starch, the iodine will turn it black or purple.

16. Repeat Steps 14 and 15 with Powder B and Powder C. When you are finished, rinse out the eye dropper. Record what you observed in Table 2.

17. Repeat Steps 14 and 15 with each of the powders, adding 1–2 drops of vinegar this time. Add your observations to Table 2. If the powder is a base, the acidic vinegar will mix with it and form fizzling carbon dioxide gas.

Troubleshooter's Guide

Below is a common problem that may arise during this experiment, a possible cause, and a way to remedy the problem.

Problem: All of the powders reacted the same in the tests.

Possible cause: Your samples might have become contaminated if the spoon, dish, and eye dropper were not cleaned before each test. This contamination will affect your test results. Try the experiment again, being careful to keep your equipment clean.

Summary of Results

Compare the results in Table 2 with the characteristics in Table 1. Can you use your test results to establish the identity of each powder? Then pick up each dish of powder and read the label on the bottom. Were you correct? Write a paragraph summarizing your findings and explaining whether they support your hypothesis.

Change the Variables

You can vary this experiment in these ways:

- Use other powders, such as salt, granulated sugar, or powdered sugar.
- Set up the experiment for someone else, perhaps a younger student, and see if he or she can identify a mystery powder you have selected.
- With an adult's help, place a sample of baking soda, cornstarch, and flour, separately, on a square of aluminum foil and heat the sample with a candle. Notice which powders melt and which turn black. Use this information to help identify mystery powders.
- Mix each powder with a little water and test it with red and blue litmus (pH) paper. If the powder is acidic, blue litmus paper will turn red. If the powder is basic, red litmus paper will turn blue. If the paper does not change color, the powder is neutral. This test provides one more characteristic to help identify the powders.

Experiment 2
Using the Scientific Method: Do fruit flies appear out of thin air?

Purpose/Hypothesis

In this experiment, you will test Aristotle's assumption that fruit flies are created spontaneously—from nothing. You will determine whether the flies are present in all air and can appear anywhere or whether they are attracted from other places by rotting fruit.

First, form a hypothesis about the outcome of this experiment based on your understanding of fruit flies and bananas, the fruit you will use in this experiment.

A hypothesis should explain these things:

- the topic of the experiment
- the variable you will change

What Are the Variables?

Variables are anything that might affect the results of an experiment. Here are the main variables in this experiment:

- the ripeness of the banana slices (this variable will be controlled by taking all the slices from the same banana)

- the temperature of the air around both sets of banana slices (flies are more active in warm temperatures)

- whether the container with the experimental slices is tightly sealed

- the opportunity for flies to be attracted to the fruit (in a sealed, air-conditioned room, flies are unlikely to be near enough to be attracted to the bananas)

The independent variable, the one you will change, is whether the bananas are in a sealed container or exposed to the air around them. The dependent variable, the one you will measure, is the presence or absence of fruit flies.

- the variable you will measure
- what you expect to happen

A hypothesis should be brief, specific, and measurable. It must be something you can test through observation. Your experiment will prove or disprove whether your hypothesis is correct. Here is a possible hypothesis for this experiment, one that Aristotle thought was true: "Fruit flies will appear on bananas even if they are kept in a covered container."

In your experiment, you will place several slices of a ripe banana in a covered container. As a control experiment, you will leave several other slices of the same banana exposed to the air. If flies appear on both the covered and the exposed banana slices, you will know that your hypothesis is correct.

Level of Difficulty
Easy/moderate.

Materials Needed
- 1 very ripe banana, unpeeled, with no obvious rotten spots
- clear container that can be completely sealed
- small, shallow bowl
- table knife
- magnifying lens
- water for cleaning the banana
- a warm, shaded area outside (or a warm area inside that is near a window or door)

Approximate Budget
$0 to $5; materials should be available in the average household.

Timetable
15 minutes to set up; five minutes to record observations each day for a week to 10 days.

How to Experiment Safely
Ask permission before beginning this experiment, as it is likely to attract flies. Handle the table knife with caution.

Step-by-Step Instructions

1. Gently rinse the unpeeled banana to clean off any fly eggs that might already be on it.

2. Peel the banana, and use the table knife to cut it into about ten slices.

3. Put half of the slices in the clear container and seal it tightly.

4. Put the rest of the slices in the uncovered, shallow dish.

Steps 3 and 4: Place five banana slices in a covered container, and five slices in an uncovered container.

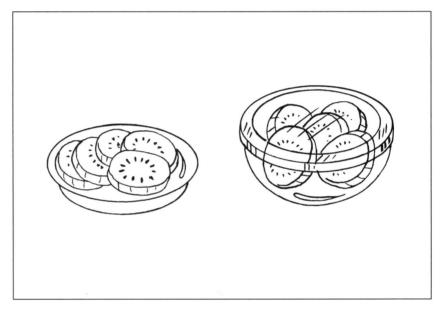

Step 6: Observe containers for the presence of fruit flies.

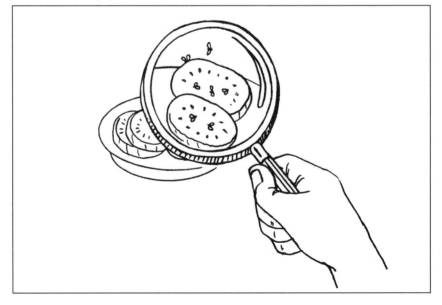

experiment
CENTRAL

Table 3
Appearance of Fruit Flies

	Day 1	Day 2	Day 3	Day 4	Day 5	Day 6	Day 7
sealed container							
open container							

5. Place the sealed container and the shallow dish in a warm, shady spot, outside if possible.

Table 3 for Experiment 2.

6. Starting the next day, use the magnifying lens to check for fruit

Troubleshooter's Guide

Below are some problems that may arise during this experiment, some possible causes, and ways to remedy the problems.

Problem: Flies appeared on the slices in the sealed container.

Possible cause: The banana must have already contained fly eggs. Try the experiment again, choosing a banana that is not so ripe and rinsing it thoroughly before you start.

Problem: No flies appeared anywhere.

Possible cause: The area around your experiment is just too clean! Try placing both containers outside, if the weather is warm, or inside in a place that is well traveled. Both containers must be exposed to the same environment.

flies. Record your observations in Table 3 each day for 7 to 10 days, or until flies appear.

Summary of Results

Study the data on your table and decide whether your hypothesis was correct. Did flies appear in the sealed container? Did they appear on the slices in the shallow dish? Write a paragraph summarizing your findings and explaining whether they support your hypothesis. If your hypothesis was not supported, what did you learn?

Change the Variables

Here are some ways you can vary this experiment:

- Use a different kind of fruit or try raw meat, such as hamburger.
- Put both containers in a warmer or a cooler place to see how that affects the results of the experiment.
- Put a banana that has obvious rotten areas on it inside a sealed container to see if flies appear from eggs already on the banana.

 # Design Your Own Experiment

How to Select a Topic Relating to this Concept

You can explore many questions using the scientific method. What has always intrigued you? For example, you could use this method to see which brand of a product gets the best results, which studying techniques help you or others learn more, or how long microwave popcorn should cook in order to pop all the kernels and burn none.

Check the For More Information section and talk with your science teacher or school or community media specialist to start gathering information on questions that interest you. As you consider possible experiments, be sure to discuss them with your science teacher or another knowledgeable adult before trying them. Some materials or procedures are dangerous to use.

Steps in the Scientific Method

To do an original experiment, you need to plan carefully and think things through. Otherwise, you might not be sure which question you are answering, what you are or should be measuring, or what your findings prove or disprove.

Here are the steps in designing an experiment:

- State the purpose of—and the underlying question behind—the experiment you propose to do.
- Recognize the variables involved, and select one that will help you answer the question at hand.
- State a testable hypothesis—an educated guess about the answer to your question.
- Decide how to change the variable you selected.
- Decide how to measure your results.

Recording Data and Summarizing Results

In your unknown powder and fruit fly experiments, your raw data might include tables, drawings, or photographs of the changes you observed. If you display your experiment, make clear the question you are trying to answer, the variable you changed, the variable you measured, the results, and your conclusions. Explain what materials you used, how long each step took, and other basic information.

Related Projects

You can undertake a variety of projects related to the scientific method. For example, you might find out how much sunlight a day produces the fastest growing seedlings, which kind of software is the easiest to learn how to use, or how to speed up the life cycle of a fruit fly. Many, many of the questions that occur to you can be answered using the scientific method!

For More Information

Gardner, Robert. *Science Projects about Chemistry.* Hillside, NJ: Enslow Publishers, 1994. ❖ Describes many science projects, including separating and identifying substances and detecting unknown solids.

VanCleave, Janice. *A+ Projects in Chemistry.* New York: Wiley, 1993. ❖ Outlines many experiments and includes information about the scientific method.

budget index

Under $5

Bold type indicates volume number.

budget index

$5—$10

experiment
CENTRAL

Bold type indicates volume number.

experiment
CENTRAL

$21—$25

budget index

$26—$30

$31—$35

Bold type indicates volume number.

level of difficulty index

Easy

Easy means that the average student should easily be able to complete the tasks outlined in the project/experiment, and that the time spent on the project is not overly restrictive.

Bold type indicates volume number.

Easy/Moderate

Easy/Moderate means that the average student should have little trouble completing the tasks outlined in the project/experiment, and that the time spent on the project is not overly restrictive.

Moderate

*Moderate means that the average student should find tasks outlined in the
project/experiment challenging but not difficult, and that the time spent
project/experiment may be more extensive.*

Bold type indicates volume number.

Moderate/Difficult

Moderate/Difficult means that the average student should find tasks outlined in the project/experiment challenging, and that the time spent on the project/experiment may be more extensive.

Difficult

Difficult means that the average student will probably find the tasks outlined in the project/experiment mentally and physically challenging, and that the time spent on the project/experiment will be more extensive.

Bold type indicates volume number.

timetable index

Bold type indicates
volume number.

30-45 minutes

1 hour

2 hours

Bold type indicates volume number.

experiment
CENTRAL

3-4 weeks

2 months

4 months

Bold type indicates volume number.

timetable index

experiment
CENTRAL

general index

Bold type indicates volume number; [ill.] indicates illustration or photograph.

general index

Buoyancy **1:** 123-138, 124 [ill.], **3:** 545
Butterfly **2:** 342 [ill.]
By-products **2:** 300

C

Camera **4:** 607
Capillary action **4:** 699
Carbohydrates **3:** 421
Carbon dioxide **1:** 3
Carbon monoxide **1:** 3,
Carnivore **4:** 668
Carotene **1:** 92, **3:** 494
Catalysts **2:** 217
Caterpillar **2:** 341 [ill.]
Celestial bodies **1:** 175
Cells **1:** 49-59
Cell membrane **1:** 51
Centrifuge **3:** 404
Channel **4:** 715
Chanute, Octave **2:** 251
Cheese curd **3:** 390 [ill.]
Chemicals **1:** 1,
Chemical energy **1:** 61-74, **3:** 509
Chemical properties **1:** 75
Chemical reaction **1:** 61, 75, 77 [ill.]
Chlorophyll **1:** 91-104, 265, **3:** 493
Chloroplasts **1:** 52, 91, **3:** 493
Chromatography **1:** 93
Cleavage **3:** 533
Climate **4:** 745
Clouds **4:** 748 [ill.]
Coagulation **2:** 316, **3:** 405
Cohesion **4:** 697, 698 [ill.]
Colloid **3:** 403
Combustion **1:** 62, **2:** 300
Complete metamorphosis **2:** 341
Compost pile **1:** 106 [ill.], 107 [ill.]
Composting **1:** 105-121
Compression **4:** 635
Concave **3:** 433
Concentration **3:** 445
Condense/condensation **4:** 729
Conduction **2:** 323
Conductors **4:** 615
Confined aquifer **2:** 308, 310 [ill.]
Coniferous trees **1:** 36 [ill.]

Constellations **4:** 604
Continental drift **4:** 684
Control experiment **1:** 2, **3:** 560
Convection **2:** 325, 326 [ill.]
Convection current **2:** 326, **4:** 684
Convex **3:** 433
Corona **1:** 177
Cotyledon **2:** 265
Crust **3:** 528
Current **4:** 615
Cyanobacteria **1:** 23
Cycles **1:** 175
Cytology **1:** 50
Cytoplasm **1:** 51 [ill.], 51

D

Darwin, Charles **4:** 647, 647 [ill.], 667
Da Vinci, Leonardo **2:** 249 [ill.]
Decanting **3:** 404
Decibel(dB) **4:** 590
Decomposition **1:** 75, 108
Decomposition reaction **1:** 76
Density **1:** 123-138, 124 [ill.], **3:** 542, **4:** 746
Detergent between water and grease **4:** 700 [ill.]
Dependent variable **3:** 560
Desert **1:** 35
Dewpoint **4:** 729
Dicot **1:** 56 [ill.]
Diffraction **2:** 360
Diffraction grating **2:** 363
Diffusion **3:** 445-459
Disinfection **2:** 316
Dissolved oxygen (DO) **1:** 139-158
Distillation **3:** 404
DNA (deoxyribonucleic acid) **1:** 51 [ill.], 52
Domains **3:** 369, 370 [ill.]
Dormancy **1:** 20, **2:** 263
Drought **2:** 232
Drum **4:** 590 [ill.]
Dry cell **2:** 187
Dust Bowl **2:** 232
Dynamic equilibrium **3:** 447

Bold type indicates volume number.

general index

H

Halley, Edmond **1**: 176
Heat **1**: 61, 323-339
Heat energy **2**: 323
Helium balloon **3**: 446 [ill.]
Herbivore **4**: 668
Hertz (Hz) **4**: 589
Heterotrophs **1**: 23
High air pressure **4**: 762
H.M.S. Challenger **3**: 542 [ill.]
Hooke, Robert **1**: 49
Hormone **4**: 648, 666
Hot air balloon **2**: 325 [ill.]
Humidity **4**: 745
Humus **1**: 105, 107
Hutton, James **3**: 527, 528 [ill.]
Hydrogen peroxide **2**: 221 [ill.]
Hydrologic cycle **4**: 713, 729
Hydrologists **4**: 730
Hydrology **4**: 729
Hydrometer **3**: 543
Hydrophilic **4**: 699
Hydrophobic **4**: 699
Hydrotropism **4**: 649
Hypertonic solution **3**: 447
Hypotonic solution **3**: 447

I

Igneous rock **3**: 528
Immiscible **1**: 125
Impermeable **2**: 307
Impurities **2**: 316
Incomplete metamorphosis **2**: 341
Independent variable **3**: 560
Indicator **3**: 479
Inertia **2**: 278
Infrared radiation **2**: 291, 326
Ingenhousz, Jan **3**: 493, 494 [ill.]
Inner core **3**: 528
Inorganic **2**: 233
Insulation/insulator **2**: 185, 291, **4**: 615
Interference fringes **2**: 359
Ions **1**: 1, 185, 403, 477
Ionic conduction **2**: 185
Isobars **4**: 762
Isotonic solutions **3**: 447

J

Janssen, Hans **1**: 49

K

Kinetic energy **3**: 509-525
Kuhne, Willy **2**: 217

L

Landfills **1**: 105-121, 108 [ill.]
Langley, Samuel Pierpont **2**: 251
Larva **2**: 341
Lava **3**: 528, 529 [ill.], 683
Leaves **1**: 92, 93 [ill.]
Leeuwenhoek, Anton van **1**: 49, 387
Lens **1**: 49, 50 [ill.]
Lichens **1**: 22 [ill.], 22
Life cycles **2**: 341-356
Lift **2**: 250
Light **2**: 357
Lightening **4**: 618 [ill.]
Light-year **4**: 604
Lilienthal, Otto **2**: 250 [ill.]
Lind, James **3**: 420 [ill.]
Lippershey, Hans **1**: 49
Litmus paper **3**: 479
Local Group, The **4**: 606
Lockyer, Joseph Norman **1**: 178 [ill.]
Low air pressure **4**: 762
Luminescence **1**: 79
Lunar eclipse **1**: 177 [ill.]
    partial lunar eclipse **1**: 178
    total lunar eclipse **1**: 177
Luster **3**: 533

M

Macroorganisms **1**: 106
Magma **3**: 528, 684
Magma chambers **4**: 684
Magma surge **4**: 686
Magnet **3**: 370 [ill.]
Magnetic circuit **3**: 371
Magnetic field **2**: 203, **3**: 369
Magnetic resonance imaging (MRI) **2**: 205 [ill.]
Magnetism **3**: 369-385
Mantle **3**: 528

Bold type indicates volume number.

general index

Bold type indicates volume number.